From Louise Bourgeois to Jeff Wall

Portraits & Studio Stills by
Elfie Semotan

Roberto Ohrt

Am Rand des Ateliers

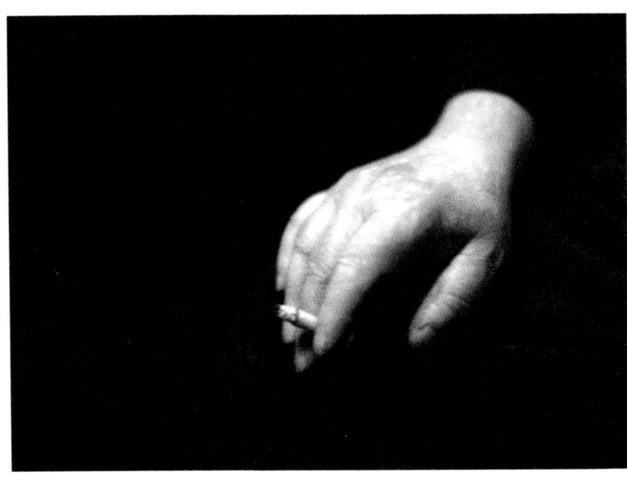

1995 **Bruno Gironcoli**
Wien/Vienna

Als Elfie Semotan im letzten Jahr, 2009, eine kleine Auswahl ihrer Künstlerporträts erstmals in Wien präsentierte, war auf der Einladungskarte keine der ausgestellten Fotografien zu sehen. Eins der Porträts für die Einladung zu nehmen, wäre wohl verlockend gewesen und wahrscheinlich sogar besonders werbewirksam, denn immerhin gab es darunter einige Aufnahmen, die mittlerweile einen gewissen Bekanntheitsgrad erreicht haben (ohne dass die Öffentlichkeit tatsächlich realisiert, wer sie gemacht hat). Außerdem sind einige der Persönlichkeiten, die Elfie Semotan schon vor Jahren aufgesucht hat, zwischenzeitlich zu lokalen Berühmtheiten oder internationalen Stars geworden, Gesichter, die das schwerfällige Interesse der Medien eher in Bewegung bringen … Wen aber hätte sie zum Fürsprecher oder Lockvogel für die anderen erheben sollen? In dieser Richtung gab es keine haltbare Lösung; alle Fragen und möglichen Entscheidungen führten letztlich in die Irre, und so fand sie einen anonymen Stellvertreter, ein Zeichen, das Individualität signalisiert und dennoch ohne Gesicht auskommt, ein klassisches Motiv aus der Porträtmalerei zudem: die ruhende Hand als helle Form auf dunklem Grund. Dieses Zeichen erinnert gleichzeitig an eine andere Frage, die unmittelbar mit den Entstehungsbedingungen ihrer Bilder zu tun hat, die Frage nach dem Verhältnis von Kunst und Fotografie. Immerhin war Elfie Semotan stets zu Leuten gegangen, die in ihrem Leben mehr oder weniger unbestritten die Orientierung der Wahrnehmung und den Weg zum Bild bestimmen. Bei ihnen erschien sie mit dem Apparat in der Hand, mit ihrer „Beobachtung" als Fotografin und einem Auftrag, der nur bedeuten konnte, dass die eigene Bildproduktion an diesem Tag an zweiter Stelle stand.

In der Malerei war die Hand, neben dem Gesicht, jenes zweite entscheidende Element, das zur Gestaltung der Individualität einer Person in Szene gesetzt werden konnte, als ein körperlicher Reflex der inneren Bewegung, der Präsenz, Schönheit oder Bereitschaft, sich anschauen zu lassen, Ausdruck von Gelassenheit und Grazie oder Eleganz, des Umgangs mit der Situation also, die für einen Moment das eigene Handeln zurückzunehmen verlangt. Die gespannte Ruhe macht die Hand auch zu einem schweigenden Vermittler oder zu einem Medium der Identifikation, der notwendigen Übertragung, die zwischen dem Maler und seinem „Gegenstand" stattfinden muss. So wird die gemalte Hand zum Reflex der anderen, die an dem Bild malt und ihrerseits – obwohl in Bewegung – immer mit der „Ruhe" kommuniziert. Insofern war das klassische Motiv – als Zitat *und* Fotografie – nicht einfach nur die Hand eines Künstlers, den wir natürlich benennen können. In der Ausstellung fehlte das Foto sogar; umso mehr war es wie eine Signatur eingesetzt, niedergelegt als Zeichen für den Kontrakt zwischen Künstler und Fotografin, um nicht zu beantworten, wer für die Entstehung des Bildes verantwortlich ist, wessen Bewegung letztlich am Auslöser entscheidend war.

Elfie Semotan hat in den letzten knapp dreißig Jahren im Austausch mit Künstlern und Künstlerinnen eine beachtliche Reihe sehr unterschiedlicher Bilder gemacht. Die Auswahl, die für das vorliegende Buch getroffen wurde, bietet einen durchaus repräsentativen Querschnitt, was eigentlich nicht betont werden muss, da es sich bei einem umfassenden Buchprojekt von selbst versteht. In diesem Fall liegen die Dinge jedoch etwas anders, denn zusammengefasst zum handlichen Format eines Bildbandes wirkt das Panorama des Ganzen noch stärker; es entfaltet sich beim Durchblättern wie ein unberechenbar wechselhaftes Kaleidoskop, voller Extreme, Kontraste und Überraschungen. Ein identifizierbares Gesicht wechselt mit Unkenntlichem, Bekanntes mit Geheimnis-

Roberto Ohrt

At the Edge of the Stu-dio

From the German by Jeanne Haunschild

When Elfie Semotan presented a small selection of her artist photographs last year, in 2009, in Vienna for the first time, not one of the exhibited photos graced the invitation that was sent out. To display one of the portraits on the invitation card would have been tempting and probably even promotionally effective, for some of her prints have in the meantime achieved a certain degree of fame (without the public actually being aware of who took them). In addition, several of the people whom Elfie Semotan had sought out years ago have meanwhile become local heroes or international stars, faces that are able to set the sluggish interest of the media in motion ... But who would deserve being elevated to spokesman—or decoy—for all the rest? There was no tenable solution to the problem; all questions and possible decisions ended in disarray. So she instead found an anonymous placeholder, a sign that proclaims individuality and yet gets by without a face and, moreover, is a classical motif of portrait painting: a reposing hand as a bright shape against a dark ground. This sign at the same time recalls another question that has to do directly with the conditions under which her photos come about, the question of the relationship between art and photography. After all, Elfie Semotan has always approached people who during their lifetime have made the *picture*, more or less indisputably, the determining factor in the orientation of their perception. She appeared before them with camera in hand, with her "observing" photographic eye, and with a mission that could only mean that their own production on that day was to take second place.

In painting it was the hand, next to the face, that was the second decisive element that could be used to set a person's individuality in scene as the physical reflex of an inner drive, as the presence, beauty or willingness to be looked at, as an expression of serenity, graciousness or elegance, in other words as a way of dealing with the situation that requires one to hold back one's own actions for a moment. The tense repose also turns the hand into a silent mediator or medium of identification and into the necessary transference that must take place between the painter and his "subject". In this way the painted hand becomes a reflection of the hand painting the picture and, for its part—although in motion—always communicates with the "repose". To this extent the classical motif—as quotation *and* photograph—is not simply the hand of an artist, whom we could naturally name. And indeed this photo was not even in the exhibition; rather, it was used as a signature, set down as a sign of the contract between artist and photographer, so as not to reveal who was responsible for the genesis of the picture or whose movement was decisive in the end when the shutter was released.

In the course of almost thirty years, Elfie Semotan has produced a notable series of very varied photographs in collaboration with artists. The selection made for the present book offers a representative cross-section of these works, which need not be stressed since it is self-evident in a comprehensive book project. In this case, however, things are somewhat different, for, brought together in the convenient format of a picture book, the panoramic scope of the photographs is even more in evidence; page after page they unfold like an unpredictable, ever-changing kaleidoscope, full of extremes, contrasts and surprises. An identifiable face gives way to an unfamiliar one, the well-known person to a mysterious one, a dramatic gesture to a vapid one—sometimes the sequence turns into a masquerade that brings us to the edge of the stage before shifting backdrops, pithy scenes and changing moods.

vollem, eine dramatische Geste mit Leere – manchmal wird der Ablauf zu einem Maskenspiel, das uns an den Rand einer Bühne stellt, vor wechselnde Räume, prägnante szenische Einheiten und Stimmungen. Leicht könnte sich der Auftritt eines jeden Einzelnen in der dichten Folge abschleifen und entwerten, doch genau das Gegenteil passiert. Jede Person erweitert mit ihrem Beitrag das Spektrum und intensiviert eine Spannung, die vor allem von Individuen handelt, was natürlich mit den „Künstlerpersönlichkeiten" zu tun hat, um die es hier geht, aber auch mit der Fotografin, da sie es vermeidet, ihren Bildern Wiedererkennungswerte, so etwas wie eine Handschrift oder einen markanten Stil, aufzuprägen; Lifestyle-Feeling wäre da zur Zeit sehr beliebt, oder eine musterhafte intellektuelle Konzeption. Stattdessen sucht sie jedes Mal neue Mittel, zugunsten der Individualität ihrer Gastgeber und im Vertrauen auf die eigene Stimmung, die Lust am Experiment oder am Element der Neugier.

Trotzdem gibt es einige Merkmale oder Bedingungen, die – wenn auch im Hintergrund – die „Hand" der Fotografin zeigen und als ein wiederkehrender Ausdruck das Ganze bestimmen. Elfie Semotan zieht es beispielsweise vor, die unmittelbare Spannung der Situation, die Reaktion auf ihre Anwesenheit, sichtbar zu halten. Bilder, die von außen an das Geschehen herantreten, sind eher selten, das Porträt der **Chapman-Brüder** etwa; es beobachtet sie im Verhalten nebeneinander, an einem Tisch mit ein paar unfertigen Dingen, Material, das die beiden Künstler vielleicht verwenden könnten und gleichzeitig oder parallel, doch sehr unterschiedlich angehen. Auch **Jenny Holzer** nimmt genau genommen keinen Kontakt zur Kamera auf, bleibt ihr allerdings nahe, sitzt da so ungerührt direkt vor der Fotografin, dass der abgewandte Blick sie zunächst ganz eindeutig als selbstbewusste Person zeichnet, aktiv, erfolgreich, eine typische New Yorkerin wahrscheinlich, bis in dieser Unabhängigkeit eine Spur von Verlassenheit aufkommt oder Einsamkeit sogar, eine leichte Kälte, wie der Wind, der ihr Haar durchzieht und nur streng bemessen Bewegung am eigenen Gesicht zulässt. Wie plakativ und unmittelbar dagegen die verkleidete **Vanessa Beecroft**: Sie scheint unter ihrer Perücke so viel Schutz gefunden zu haben, dass sie das Versteckspiel mit einem knalligen Lachen noch übertönen will. Oder **Raymond Pettibon**, der seinen Hund zur Kamera hinhält und die Konfrontation denkbar einfach aufhebt, und dann mit einer Freundlichkeit da ist, überraschend aufmerksam, zugänglich, ein Überschuss an Offenheit in diesem Augenblick, eine unkomplizierte Hilfsbereitschaft, die viele, die ihn oder seine Kunst zu kennen glauben, mit seiner „Künstlerperson" wohl nicht verbinden würden. Ganz anders wiederum **Christopher Wool**: Einerseits will er wohl im Schatten an der Wand seiner Bilder bleiben; sie sind bekanntlich wie robuste Schilde einer ungeschützten Öffentlichkeit angelegt, und sie könnten ihm im rauen Medium der Fotografie sogar helfen; so scheint es jedenfalls. Denn andererseits kann er offenbar auch dort nicht stehen, womöglich für seine eigenen Produkte herhalten oder sie als die verantwortliche Person verdrängen, und das ist dann der Moment des Porträts, des Versuchs, sich aus der nächsten Funktion zu lösen. Kein Vergleich mit dem, was **Jason Rhoades** vor der Kamera im Angebot hat: draußen in der Wüste, zufrieden in der extremen Landschaft, unbekümmert im Freien und verspielt in seiner Geste am Gatter, jener klassischen Figur des amerikanischen Westens, die er doch so lässig und gekonnt wie ein Profi nutzt, um gegenüber der Sonne seine Augen im Schatten zu halten.

In diesem Zusammenhang – es waren nun zunächst überwiegend Schwarzweiß-Aufnahmen – nimmt das Porträt von **Martin Kippenberger** eine besondere Stellung ein ... nicht jedoch, weil es farbig ist; das ging gar nicht anders, denn er trägt ein buntes Sommerkleid, und ein solches Detail darf die Fotografie natürlich

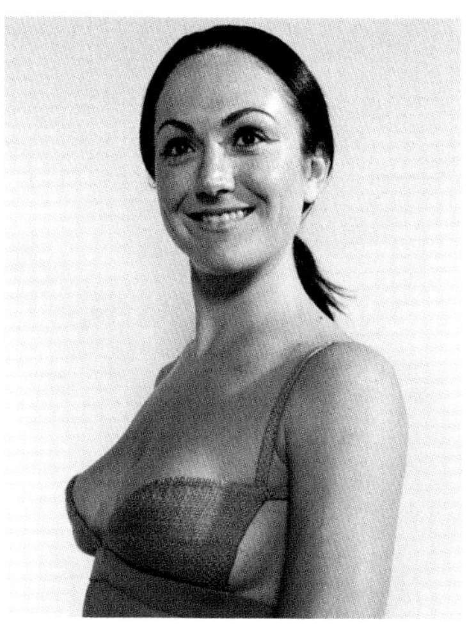

1999 **Vanessa Beecroft**
New York

Elfie Semotan hat in den letzten knapp **dreißig Jahren** im Austausch mit **Künstlern** und **Künstlerinnen** eine beachtliche Reihe sehr unterschiedlicher **Bilder** gemacht.

It could easily happen that the appearance of one individual after the other would have a wearying and wearing down effect, but precisely the opposite happens. The contribution of each person broadens the spectrum and intensifies the tension emanating from individuals—which above all has to do with the fact that the portraits are of outstanding "artistic personalities", but also has to do with the photographer herself, since she avoids elaborating a signature style that would make her photos immediately recognizable: a "lifestyle feeling", for instance, would be very popular at the moment or perhaps an exemplary intellectual concept. Instead, for each occasion she seeks new means that favour the individuality of her hosts while relying on her own feeling at the moment, her delight in experimentation or in the element of curiosity.

Nevertheless, there are a number of distinguishing features or conditions that—even if kept to the background—show the "hand" of the photographer and identify the oeuvre as a recurring artistic expression. For instance, Elfie Semotan prefers to let the immediate tension arising from the situation, the reaction to her presence, remain visible. Pictures that approach the scene of events from without are rather seldom, like the portrait of the Chapman brothers; it observes their behaviour next to each other, at a table with a couple of unfinished things, material that the two artists will perhaps be willing to use, while going about it, at the same time or parallel to one another, in very different ways. Nor does Jenny Holzer, in a strict sense, have any contact with the camera, although remaining close to it. Sitting directly in front of the photographer, she is so unmoved that her averted eyes at first appear to reveal her as a self-confident, active, successful, no doubt typical New Yorker, until a trace of forlornness or even loneliness suddenly appears in the midst of this seeming independence, a slight coldness like the wind that ruffles her hair and allows only a strictly measured movement of her features. How bold and direct, by contrast, the masqueraded Vanessa Beecroft: under her wig she seems to feel so protected that she wants to drown out this hide-and-seek game with brash laughter. Or Raymond Pettibon, who holds up his dog to the camera, thus neutralizing the confrontation in a conceivably simple way, and then presents himself with such friendliness as surprisingly attentive and accessible, with a lavish openness at the moment, an uncomplicated cooperativeness that many who think they know him or his art would not necessarily associate with his "artistic personality". Quite different, in turn, is Christopher Wool: on the one hand he wants to remain in the shadows at the wall with his pictures; they are famously laid out like robust shields before an unguarded public, and they could even help him in the raw medium of photography; at least it seems so. But, on the other hand, he can obviously also not stand there, possibly serving as a stand-in for his own products or supplanting them as the person responsible for them. And that is the moment of the portrait, the attempt to free himself from the next operation. No comparison with what Jason Rhoades has to offer the camera: out in the desert, content in the extreme countryside, easy-going in the open air and playful in his gesture at the gate, a classical figure of the American West, a pose he adopts with the nonchalance and skill of a professional in order to keep his eyes in the shade opposite the sun.

In this context—up to now the shots were predominantly in black-and-white—the portrait of Martin Kippenberger occupies a special position ... not however because it is in colour; it wouldn't have worked any other way, for he is wearing a brightly coloured summer dress, and such a detail cannot be overlooked by the camera. Colour does not make artistic design in photography any easier and yet—or perhaps because of this—the picture has turned into an unusual example of the tension characteristic of all of Elfie Semotan's portraits. It all came about out of an exaggeration not quite seriously meant, a humorous remark aiming to alleviate the stress ("Why don't we simply take Martin", namely a man as model), and then: no sooner said than done, the situation was so intriguingly brought to a climax by the summoned performer that the photographer

In the course of almost **thirty years, Elfie Semotan** has produced a notable series of very varied **photographs** in collaboration with **artists.**

Elfie Semotan zeigt ihre Porträts eigentlich nie ohne jene anderen Fotos, die sie am Tag des Besuchs bei den Künstlern gewissermaßen nebenher noch gemacht hat.

nicht übergehen. Farbe macht die künstlerische Gestaltung in der Fotografie keineswegs leichter und dennoch – oder gerade deshalb – wird das Bild zu einem ungewöhnlichen Beispiel für die Spannung, die alle Porträts von Elfie Semotan auszeichnet. Entstanden aus einer nicht ganz ernst gemeinten Übertreibung, einer lustigen Bemerkung zur Entspannung („Warum nehmen wir nicht einfach Martin", also den Mann, als Mannequin), und dann ohne Umschweife hergestellt, wurde die Situation vom herbeigerufenen Darsteller derart verblüffend zugespitzt, dass die Fotografin am Ende selbst verwundert war, obwohl sie das Ganze genau so angelegt und gewollt hatte. Im Grunde macht das Bild die Spannungen gar nicht mal deutlicher oder sichtbar, sondern vielmehr besonders *spürbar*. Es ist aus einem starken Kontrast aufgebaut, der doch nur indirekt erscheint; es bleibt ein Rätsel, das sich als Rätsel nicht zu erkennen gibt, getarnt als auffällige Übertretung, die dem Anschein der Deutlichkeit einen unidentifizierbaren Zusatz beimischt.

Martin Kippenberger durchschritt besonders schnell den Augenblick der Annäherung, den die Situation des Auftritts vor der Kamera verlangt, ein Problem, das oft hinderlich ist, bei Künstlern – so Elfie Semotan – jedoch meistens nicht. Sie wissen, dass sie ihren Stoff nicht so nehmen dürfen, wie er sich im ersten Moment anbietet, und dieses Wissen bringen sie sofort ein. Außerdem kannte **Martin Kippenberger** das Posing vor der Kamera seit seiner Kindheit. Selbstporträts waren ein Teil seiner Kunst, und wie kaum ein anderer beherrschte er solche Spielereien, liebte sie, ließ auf diesem Gebiet immer neue Sachen geschehen, benutzte sich selbst dafür als Instrument. Eine Vorführung der eigenen Person, den Mann in Frauenkleidern geben – er hatte es in den 1980er Jahren schon einmal gemacht, mit dem ärmlichen Charme einer anatolischen Immigrantin; heute ist das natürlich nicht mehr wirklich riskant oder bestenfalls, wenn die abgetragene Geste als eine solche ins Bild kommt. Vielleicht hängt das grelle, schöne Ding deshalb an ihm herab wie ein Kleid aus Großmutters Zeiten und er selbst als ihr abgetragener Körper drunter, ein „malerisches" Stück Stoff noch dazu, an der Grenze zur Stimmung „kreativ sein und glücklich werden". Und diese Lust an Farbe verrät auch der dunkle Teint, den der Künstler ernst und verhalten hinzugibt, als seinen rauen Schatten zum bunten Augenblick. Die Gegensätze sind also leicht benannt, was aber hält sie zusammen?

In der Kunst, vor allem, seit sie sich als ein Teil der Massenkultur begreifen muss, fallen extreme Individualität und öffentliche Rückmeldung über das Leben der Ausnahmefigur nicht nur ziemlich regelmäßig (oder voraussehbar zuverlässig) auseinander; die künstlerische Botschaft kommt nicht selten als monströses Zerrbild vom Publikum zum Entsender zurück: „Genie", „Malerfürst", „Grande Dame" ... eine feudale Ruinenlandschaft erstreckt sich da, eine ganze Reihe verstaubter Gespenster und Grabkammern des Lebens. **Jonathan Meese** aktiviert die Resonanzkatastrophen, die in diesem Zwischenreich schnell entstehen, mit unvergleichlicher Virtuosität. In übertrieben exzessiven Performances stellt er seine Person als durchgedrehten Wiedergänger all der Geister zur Verfügung, die im Publikum auf eine Verkörperung warten, Diktatoren wie Hitler und Stalin, Plakatphantome wie Charles Bronson oder Diana Rigg, Leinwandträume wie Zardoz oder Caligula. Zu dieser öffentlichen Konstruktion schafft das Porträt von Elfie Semotan eine klare Spannung, entschieden als Kontrast hergestellt und zugleich sehr erhellend: **Jonathan Meese** hat sich an die Wand gelehnt, den Rücken zum Apparat, angehalten wie für eine noch folgende experimentelle Entblößung, die auf seinen Ruf verweist (und auf seinen Stoff, den eigenen Körper), aber nicht ausgeführt wird. Sichtbar ist stattdessen eine kommunikative Struktur, eine Art Darstellung von Verständigung, ohne dass ihr Inhalt erzählt wird: der ungeschützte Rücken, der abwartende Blick, über die Schulter zur Kamera gewendet, der erhobene Arm, als ob er sich dort in der Senkrechten hinlegen wollte, ein Augenblick der Entwaffnung und Analyse, die dem Künstler und seinem künstlerischen Medium ungewöhnlich einfach, eigenständig und direkt zu ihrem Recht verhilft.

Das Porträt aus der Serie, die mit **Louise Bourgeois** entstand, verlangt einen ganz anderen Kommentar. Es ist zwar inzwischen fast so berühmt und bekannt wie die Künstlerin selbst, stellt aber einen ungewöhnlichen Sonderfall dar. Die Bildhauerin hat den öffentlichen Auftritt eher vermieden und entsprechend wenige Auf-

Elfie Semotan almost never shows her **portraits** without the **other photos** that she takes as a **sideline,** as it were, on the day of her visit.

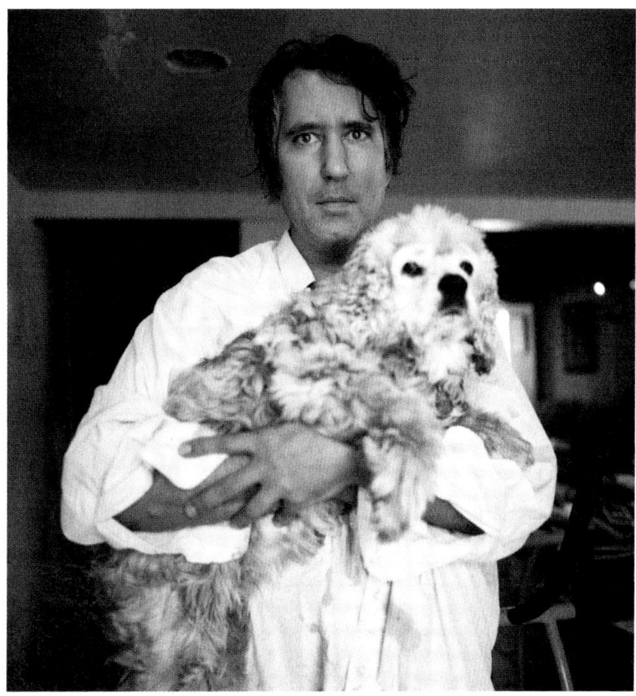

2001 **Raymond Pettibon**
Los Angeles

herself was astonished in the end, although she was the one who had arranged the whole thing and she had wanted it this way. Basically, the photo does not make the tension much clearer or more visible, but rather especially *tangible*. It has been built up out of a strong contrast, which, however, appears only indirectly. It remains an enigma that doesn't reveal itself as an enigma, disguised as it is as a striking transgression that mixes some unidentifiable additive into the semblance of explicitness.

Martin Kippenberger passed very quickly through the moment of convergence required in the situation of appearing before the camera, a problem that is often an impediment, but with artists mostly not, according to Elfie Semotan. They know they must not take their material as it presents itself in this first moment, and this is knowledge they immediately utilize. Besides, Martin Kippenberger has been posing in front of cameras since childhood. Self-portraits have always been part of his art, and like hardly any other he was a past master at just such stunts; he loved them. In this field he always initiated new events, using himself as an instrument. A presentation of his own person, a man in women's clothes—he had already done this once in the 1980s, displaying the humble charm of an Anatolian immigrant woman. Today this is naturally no longer particularly risky or, in the best case scenario, when the overused gesture as such appears in the picture. Perhaps that is the reason the gaudy tissue hangs on him like a dress from grandmother's time and he himself as her worn-out body under it, moreover an even "painterly" piece of fabric bordering on the sentiment of "be creative and become happy". And this delight in colour is also revealed in the dark complexion that the artist adds gravely and cautiously as the raw shadow to the bright moment. The opposites are thus easy to name, but what holds them together?

In art, above all since it has had to understand itself as part of mass culture, there is fairly regularly (or predictably often) a gulf between extreme individuality and public feedback about the life of the exceptional figure; not seldom the artistic message comes back from public to sender as a monstrous distortion: "Genius", "Painter Prince", "Grande Dame"—a grandiose expanse of ruins abounds, a whole series of fusty ghosts and sepulchres of life. With incomparable virtuosity, Jonathan Meese activates the resonating catastrophes that quickly arise in this in-between realm. In exorbitantly excessive performances, he puts his own person like a lunatic zombie at the disposal of all the ghosts who are waiting for their reincarnation in the audience, dictators like Hitler and Stalin, poster phantoms like Charles Bronson or Diana Rigg, screen dreams like Zardoz or Caligula. In her portrait of this public construct Elfie Semotan deliberately creates a tension as contrast and, at the same time, as enlightenment: Jonathan Meese is leaning against the wall, his back to the camera, pausing as if readying himself for some still-to-follow experimental revelation, one which points to his reputation (and to his material medium, his own body), but then is not carried out. What is instead visible is a communicative structure, a kind of portrayal of mutual exchange, but without revealing what it is about: his vulnerable back, his wait-and-see glance over his shoulder towards the camera, his raised arm, as though he wanted to lie flat against the vertical wall; a disarming and analytic moment that helps the artist and his artistic medium in an unusually easy, independent and direct way to come into their own.

The portrait from the series on Louise Bourgeois requires a completely different commentary. Although it is meanwhile almost as famous and well-known as the artist herself, it represents an out-of-the-ordinary special case. The sculptress

nahmen gibt es von ihr. Die Session mit Elfie Semotan gehört also zu den absoluten Ausnahmen. Davon ist in den Porträts allerdings nichts zu spüren; im Gegenteil: Die Künstlerin wirkt ungemein sicher, wie jemand, der sich mit diesem Moment auskennt und genau weiß, welche Haltung notwendig ist, worauf es ankommt. Gelassen, unbeirrt, wenn nicht sogar majestätisch schaut sie in die Kamera, wie gegen die Sonne und mit einem Lächeln für das grelle Licht ... wenn es denn ein Lächeln ist und nicht vielmehr ein entschiedenes Schweigen, das zu den selbstverständlichen Gesten der Hände hinüberlenkt und den Augenblick in der Zeit einnimmt, die auf dem Bild nicht angehalten, in der Welt hinter ihren Augen aber ganz anders dahinzulaufen scheint.

Elfie Semotan zeigt ihre Porträts eigentlich nie ohne jene anderen Fotos, die sie am Tag des Besuchs bei den Künstlern gewissermaßen nebenher noch gemacht hat. Während die Porträts, der eigentliche Anlass der Reise, eher im kleinen oder mittleren Format ausgestellt werden, bevorzugt sie für die Atelieraufnahmen große Abzüge – sie haben also ganz entschieden ihr Gewicht, das gleichwohl in seinen Grenzen bleibt, denn von dieser Art Stillleben sind immer deutlich weniger zu sehen. Der Blick ins Atelier rekonstruiert die Bedingungen der Sitzung ohne die Person und wirkt zunächst wie eine ziellose Abschweifung zur Seite, was natürlich nicht stimmt, ihm als eine Schwingung aber erhalten bleibt. Elfie Semotan hat die leere Szenerie am Rand des Geschehens als ein Teil des Ganzen wahrgenommen und dann bewusst festgehalten; sie hat dort ein Potential entdeckt, eine unausgesprochene Ambivalenz, die sie ins Spiel bringen wollte. Und auch auf diesem Schauplatz kamen die Künstler ihr entgegen, mit dem Unbestimmten, der Unordnung oder einem idyllischen Detail, extrem professionell und beiläufig in der Vermeidung all der Standards, die in unserer Zeit so flüssig geworden sind, dass kaum noch auffällt, wie sehr ihr Regelwerk uns und unsere Bilder verhärtet. Das ist der Beitrag der Künstler, hergestellt in der Form ihres Lebens, ihrer Umgebung, ihrer Produktionsbedingungen. Ebenso wichtig und wirksam auf diesem Terrain ist aber die Fotografin, die das „Bild“ und dessen Möglichkeit sieht, das Stillleben als ein drittes Element einführt, als ein zusätzliches Feld, das die dialogische Produktion öffnet und in Bewegung bringt. Die Wirkung ist in diesem Buch unübersehbar; es ist eine aktivierende Vielfalt, Ergebnis einer beweglichen Forschung, die in dem Geflecht der Pole und Positionen – Kunst oder Fotografie, Person und Werk, Öffentlichkeit und Studio, Aktivität und Stillstand, Tradition und Ausnahme – vor allem eines herstellt: die Möglichkeit, sich selbst und dem Nächsten immer wieder anders gegenüberzutreten.

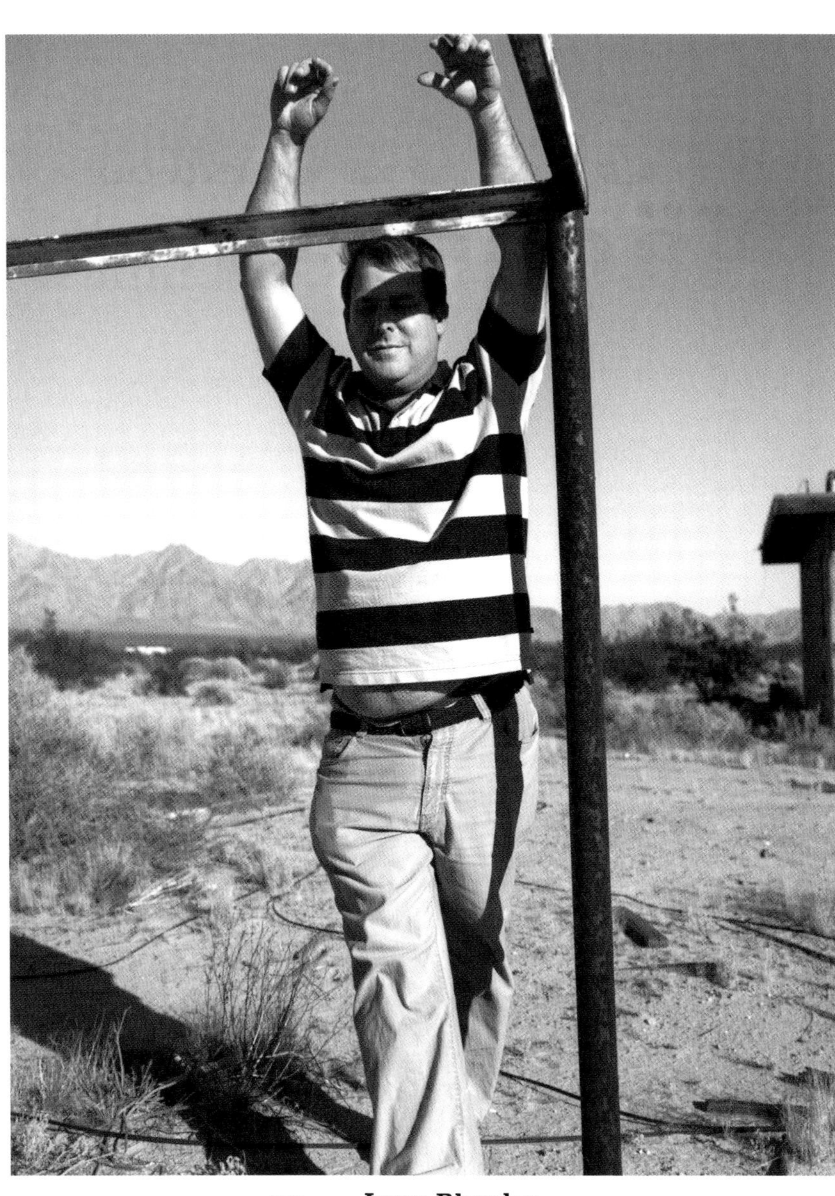

2006 **Jason Rhoades**
Palm Springs

… die Möglichkeit,
sich selbst und dem **Nächsten** immer wieder **anders gegenüber-**zutreten.

… the possibility to confront **one's own self** and **one's neighbour** again and again in a **different way.**

has tended to avoid public appearances, and correspondingly few photos exist of her. The session with Elfie Semotan was therefore an absolute exception. But nothing of this is discernible in the portraits; on the contrary. The artist seems immensely sure of herself, like someone who is familiar with this moment and knows exactly which pose is necessary and what matters. Serene, unperturbed, if not even majestic, she gazes into the camera as if against the sun and with a smile for the glaring light … if in fact it is a smile and not rather a strict silence that diverts our view to the matter-of-fact gesture of her hands and takes in the moment in time that is not arrested in the picture, but seems to be racing along quite differently in the world behind her eyes.

Elfie Semotan almost never shows her portraits without the other photos that she takes as a sideline, as it were, on the day of her visit. While the portraits—the actual reason behind the visit—are exhibited more often in small or mid-sized formats, she prefers large prints for her shots of the studios. These are therefore decidedly of considerable significance, while all the same remaining within bounds, for there are always notably fewer of this kind of still-lifes to be seen. The view into the studio reconstructs the conditions of the session minus the person and has the initial effect of a random digression off to the side, which naturally is not the case, since its vibration remains. Elfie Semotan takes in the empty scenery on the edge of the central event as a part of the whole and then consciously captures it; here she discovers a potential, an unspoken ambivalence that she has wanted to bring into play. And at this showplace, too, the artists accommodate her with something undefined, a certain disorder or an idyllic detail, while remaining extremely professional and casual in the avoidance of all standards that have become so fluent in our time so that we hardly notice how much their set of regulations hardens us and our pictures. That is the contribution the artists make, fabricated in the shape of their life, their environs, their conditions of production. However, the photographer is equally important and effective on this terrain. It is she who sees the "picture" and its possibility, introducing the still-life as a third element, an additional field that launches the dialogical production and sets it in motion. The effect in this book is immeasurably great; it is an activating diversity, the result of mobile research that in the nexus of opposite poles and positions—art or photography, person and work, public and studio, activity and standstill, tradition and exception—produces one thing above all: the possibility to confront one's own self and one's neighbour again and again in a different way.

Margit Zuckriegl

Als Person zeigen, als Bild schaffen

Die Person hinter der Kunst, der Mensch als schöpferisch Arbeitender, das künstlerische Werk und sein Produzent – seit der Renaissance interessiert den Kunstbetrachter das Individuum, das zu den Kunstwerken gehört. Erst da kristallisierte sich die Figur des Künstlers als „Auktor" heraus, wird die Vergeistigung des künstlerischen Schaffens[1] als Prozess des Interpretierens von Welt und Gesellschaft erkannt. Waren es noch bis zum Auftauchen der ersten großen Künstlerpersönlichkeiten immer das Umfeld des Handwerklichen, Meisterlichen, das die Tätigkeit des Künstlers geprägt hatte, sowie die vorgegebenen inhaltlichen Aufgabenstellungen durch Auftraggeber, so emanzipiert sich das künstlerische Schaffen zusehends bis zu einer der modernsten Künstlerpersönlichkeiten der Kunstgeschichte: Francisco de Goya – letzter Hofmaler einer bröckelnden Gesellschaftsordnung und erster Vertreter eines neuen künstlerischen Selbstverständnisses. Seine ohne imperialen oder höfisch-aristokratischen Impetus geschaffenen Werke gehören zu den ersten, denen eine „freie" Kunstausübung als Motivation zugrunde liegt, er könnte als erster „Ausstellungskünstler"[2] der Moderne bezeichnet werden. Und das *Bild* dieses neuen Typus von Künstler? Es sind vor allem die Selbstporträts, eingegliedert in den formalen und ästhetischen Kanon des jeweiligen Künstlers, die uns Auskunft über die Physiognomie, das Aussehen des Künstlers geben; damit ist eine Trennung von „Dokumentation" und „Interpretation" aufgehoben: Der Künstler sieht sich in einer Art Selbstschau, geprägt durch die Problematiken des künstlerischen Arbeitens und der Bildwerdung seiner Sicht auf sich selbst. Goya tritt uns als verschatteter Grübler entgegen, als Skeptiker, weich im Kontur und verwischt im Duktus: der Künstler, verwoben in sein Werk, Teil seiner eigenen interpretierenden Tätigkeit und seiner individuellen künstlerischen Handschrift. Diesem kritischen Selbstverständnis des Künstlers, das gezeichnet ist vom Ringen mit, vom Skeptizismus gegenüber dem eigenen Tun, tritt die Idee des Künstlers als Protagonist einer Selbstinszenierung entgegen.

Seit dem Beginn der Verwendung von fotografischen Techniken um die Mitte des 19. Jahrhunderts gehört das Genre der „Künstlerfotografie" zu einem der möglichen Anwendungsfelder der neuen Technologie. Wie sich Denker, Erfinder, Wissenschaftler, Schriftsteller in den vorgegebenen Kanon einer bourgeoisen Porträtfotografie einfügen, ist überraschend und wird nur verständlich unter den Vorzeichen einer neuen, gesellschaftlich anerkannten Stellung der künstlerischen Tätigkeit im Kontext des geistigen Lebens einer Umbruchzeit. Stabilität und Sicherheit vermitteln die nach unten breit angelegten Halbfigurenporträts in ihren graphischen Schmuckrahmen – parat fürs Lexikon und für enzyklopädische Kompendien. Eine heutige, aktuelle Porträtfotografie hat sich von einem soziologischen oder politischen Interpretationsgestus, wie etwa noch bei August Sander, gelöst und ordnet sich – wie bei Goya – dem Kontext der künstlerischen Handschrift zu; es ist nun der eigenständige fotografische Gestus, an den sich Wahrnehmung und Kritik wenden.

1 **Walter Paatz, Die Kunst der Renaissance in Italien,** Stuttgart 1953

2 **Oskar Bätschmann, Ausstellungskünstler,** Köln 1997

Margit
Zuckriegl

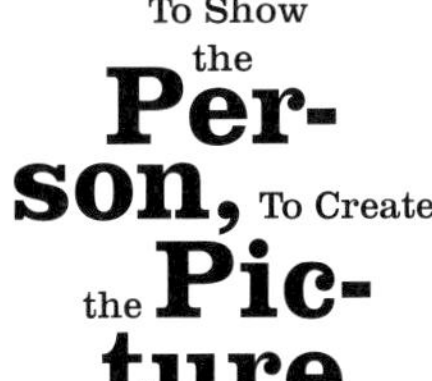

To Show the Person, To Create the Picture

From the German by
Jeanne
Haunschild

The person behind the artwork, the person as a creator, the artistic work itself and its maker—ever since the Renaissance, the viewer of art has been interested in the individual behind the artworks. It is here that the figure of the artist as "author" first materializes, that the etherealization of artistic creativity[1] is recognized as a process of interpreting the world and society. Up until the appearance of the first great personalities among the artists, it was always the environment of craftsmanship, of masterly skill, as well as the given thematic framework formulated by the art patron, that shaped the artist's work. From this time on artistic production became increasingly emancipated, crowned by the emergence of one of art history's most modern artists: Francisco de Goya—the last court painter of a crumbling social order and the first representative of a new self-understanding of the artist. Goya created works with no impetus from imperial or aristocratic court; they are among the first to be based on a "free" rendering of art as their sole motivation. In fact, Goya could be called Modernism's first "exhibition artist".[2] And what about the image of this new type of artist? It is above all their own self-portraits, incorporated into the formal and aesthetic canon of the respective individual, that provide us with information about the physiognomy of the artist, thus suspending any separation between "documentation" and "interpretation". The artist sees himself in a kind of self-observation, marked by the problems inherent in artistic work and the formulation of his view of himself. Goya appears to be brooding in the shadows, a sceptic muted in contour and blurred in brush stroke: the artist merged with his work, part of his own act of interpretation and his own artistic handwriting. Out of this critical self-conception of the artist, marked by a struggle with, and a scepticism towards, his own activity, comes the antithetical idea of the artist as the protagonist of his own self-dramatisation.

Since the first use of photographic techniques around the mid-19th century, the genre of "artist photography" has been one of the fields of application for the new technology. The way thinkers, inventors, scientists and writers blended in with the given canon of bourgeois portrait photography is surprising and only understandable in the context of the new, heightened social standing of the art profession within the intellectual life of this era of change. These broadly based half-figure portraits convey a sense of stability and security in their decorative picture frames, ready for the lexicon or encyclopaedic compendium. Present-day portrait photography has freed itself from the pretence of sociological or political interpretation, as was still practised, for instance, by August Sander, and arrays itself—as did Goya—within the context of an artistic signature; perception and critique now address themselves to the gesture of the autonomous artist.

1 **Walter Paatz,** Die Kunst der Renaissance in Italien, Stuttgart 1953

2 **Oskar Bätschmann,** Ausstellungskünstler, Cologne 1997

Der Künstler im Bild

Der künstlerische Autor wird in einer als „Künstlerfotografie" nur vage beschriebenen eigenen Typologie von Porträtfotografie zum Bildgegenstand und gleichzeitig zum möglichen Stellvertreter und Interpreten seiner künstlerischen Idee. Wenn dem so wäre, müsste man von dem Bild des Künstlers auf seine Arbeit schließen können. Gerade Fotografen, Fotografinnen wie Elfie Semotan treten den Gegenbeweis an: Ihre Fotografie ist nie bloße Porträtfotografie, ihre Künstlerbildnisse sind nie eindimensionale Ikonen einer Physiognomie; Elfie Semotans „Portraits and Studio Stills" sind verhaftet in ihrer eigenen fotografischen Bildsprache, sie sind Teil ihrer spezifischen fotografischen Produktion und fungieren damit als Werkgruppe innerhalb ihres künstlerischen Œuvres. Dass sie als Fotografin immer daran interessiert war, dem Individuellen ihrer Motive nachzuspüren und aus der Dialektik von Sehen und Abbilden eine spannungsreiche Rhetorik im Bildnerischen zu entwickeln, gehört zum Charakteristischen ihrer Arbeit. Vielfach erprobte Handlungs- und Herangehensweisen ihrer renommierten Mode- und Werbefotografie überträgt sie auf die fotografischen Bilder von Künstlern und ihren Ateliersituationen. Stabilität, Sicherheit, Abgeklärtheit sind Kriterien, die in der Welt von Semotans Fotografien nicht vorkommen; ihre Porträts zeigen die Sujets im Zustand ihrer Zeitlichkeit. Wie Skulpturen auf Zeit werden sie aus dem Hintergrund herausgelöst, nicht ohne diesen bühnenbildhaft, atmosphärisch stark miteinzubauen; Licht und Perspektive bauen geradezu das Figürliche einer Person auf, schälen sie heraus und statten sie mit plastischen Valeurs aus; Konturlinien sind das bestimmende Element ihrer Fotobildnisse, Volumina setzen sich gegen Bildfolien ab, die skulptierten Leiber runden sich und werden in einem attributiv gebrauchten Raum verortet.

„Die Person zeigen" wolle sie, schrieb Elfie Semotan an Klaus Gallwitz, „den Künstler, sein Atelier zeigen, vielleicht ein Gefühl für ihn vermitteln."[3] Diese Zeilen betrafen die Porträts und Atelierbilder ihres ersten Ehemannes, Kurt Kocherscheidt, gelten aber für all die anderen Künstlerporträts, die sie seit zwei Jahrzehnten vorlegt. Als Insiderin der Szene und Freundin vieler Künstler hat sie einen direkten Zugang zu den Ateliers und einen unkomplizierten Modus der Annäherung: Sie entwickelt mit den Künstlern gemeinsam die Konzepte für ihre Fotografien, oft in sehr intuitivem Erfassen der Werkidee des Künstlers, der Künstlerin, oft aus der jahrzehntelangen Freundschaft heraus, oft als Teil einer größeren konzeptiven Aufgabenstellung. Ihre Fotografie changiert zwischen dem Respekt vor der eigenwilligen und eigenständigen Persönlichkeit des Künstlers, seiner individuellen Örtlichkeit, die der Künstler selbst wählt, und dem fotografischen Gestus, der mit eingebracht wird. Zwischen dem Beschreiben der Persona und dem Bilden der Person liegen ihre fotografischen Gestaltungs- und Interpretationsmöglichkeiten – und hier eröffnet sich der spezifische Stil dieser Fotografin.

3 **Klaus Gallwitz (Hrsg.),** **Augen-echo, Ausst.-Kat.,** Düsseldorf 2008

The Artist in the Picture

In "artist photography", which can only be vaguely described as an independent typology of portrait photography, the artistic author becomes the picture's subject and, at the same time, the possible stand-in for, and interpreter of, his own artistic idea. If this were the case, the picture of the artist should give us an indication of his work. It is photographers like Elfie Semotan who provide evidence to the contrary. Her photographs are never just portrait photography; her photos of artists are never one-dimensional icons of a physiognomy; Elfie Semsotan's "Portraits and Studio Stills" are rooted in her own photographic vocabulary. They are part of her specific photographic production and thus operate as a work group within her artistic oeuvre. A charactristic feature of her work as a photographer is that she has always been interested in tracing the individual aspects of her motifs and in developing their image into a stimulating dialectical rhetoric of observing and depicting. The tried and tested way she goes about shooting her renowned fashion and advertising photos is a method she carries over to her photographs of artists and their studio situations. Stability, security and serenity are not criteria that exist in the world of Semotan's photography; her portraits show their subjects in the condition of their temporal existence. Like momentary sculptures, they are peeled out of their background, but not without being re-integrated into its atmospheric setting and staginess; light and perspective virtually recreate the person's figure, crystallize it and furnish it with three-dimensional qualities. Contours are the defining element of her portraits; volumes stand out against picture layers. The sculptural bodies round out and are embedded in an attributively inhabited room.

She wants "to show the person", wrote Elfie Semotan to Klaus Gallwitz, "to show the artist, his studio, perhaps convey a sense of him."[3] These lines pertain to the portraits and studio pictures of her first husband, Kurt Kocherscheidt, but are true of all the other artists' portraits that she has made in the last two decades. As an insider of the scene and a friend of many artists, she has had direct access to their studios and an uncomplicated way of approaching them: she develops the concepts for her photographs in collaboration with the individual artist, often in a very intuitive understanding of the artist's idea behind his work, often from a decades-long friendship, often as part of a larger conceptual formulation. Her photography oscillates between respect for the idiosyncratic and independent personality of the artist, the individual location that the artist himself chooses, and the photographic gesture that takes place. The photographic possibilities she has for design and interpretation lie between describing the persona and depicting the person; and here the photographer's specific style comes into play.

3 **Klaus Gallwitz (Ed.),** Augen-echo, exh. cat., Düsseldorf 2008

Der Atem des Werkes

Das Immaterielle einer künstlerischen Idee lässt sich nicht kongruent in einem Bild festhalten. Es sind deren Spuren und die temporäre Verfestigung, welche im fotografischen Bild auftauchen können – für einen Moment. Die Anwesenheit der Fotografin eröffnet für einen Augenblick die Sicht auf den Künstler, auf sein Arbeiten; der Atem des Werkes lässt sich erahnen. Niemals definiert die Fotografin den Künstler als genialisches Schöpferwesen oder kreatürlichen Demiurgen. Sie tastet die Persönlichkeit ab, lässt den Spielraum zur eigenen Interpretation von Befindlichkeit und lotet einen Tiefenraum hinter der geschilderten Person aus. Ihrer fotografischen Sprache ist das „Kippen" von Glamour in Absurdität, von affirmativer Pose in schwankende Fragilität, von effektvoller Präsenz in verwischte Abwesenheit eigen. Ihre Ausleuchtung rechnet vor, wie Volumen, Rauminhalt, Masse abzubilden sind, ihre Erzählweise löscht solche kognitiven Parameter wieder aus: Sie erzählt von schwebenden Models mit Blumen in der Hand, von einer zu Boden fallenden Künstlerin, von einem strampelnden Baby im Arm eines Malers; sie schildert das modrige Dunkel eines chaosbeladenen Atelierwinkels, den angehaltenen Stummfilm einer sich verselbständigenden Objektgruppe, den verlassenen Trailer in der Metallglut der amerikanischen Wüste.

„Ich bin nicht der, der ich zu sein scheine" ist ein Bekenntnis des Protagonisten in Manuel Vázquez Montalbáns Roman „Das Quartett",[4] in dem aus der Schilderung rund um einen Mordfall ein irrlichterndes Szenario wird. Die scheinbar so klar gezeichneten, fast skulpturhaft definierten und präsentierten Figuren kippen im Fortschreiten der Erzählung ins Ungewisse: Hinter dem Bild eines Menschen steht noch etwas, eine Idee, ein Movens, eine Intention. Wer kann dahinterblicken und wer kann das erahnen? Das Bild eines Menschen eröffnet auch immer das Bild des Nichtgezeigten – und gerade in den Porträts von Künstlern sind diese offenen Stellen, diese Gründe im Dazwischen von Bedeutung. Dies abzubilden oder in fotografische Bilder miteinzubauen, ist eine Herangehensweise, die von skrupulösem Umgang mit Person und Werk und von ingeniösem Erfassen von beidem kündet. Elfie Semotan ist eine Künstlerin, die Künstler abbildet, sie in ihrer persönlichen Handschrift skizziert, umreißt, manchmal einkreist, manchmal nur schlaglichtartig antippt; das Atmosphärische ihrer Fotobildnisse ist immer aus dem Zusammenhang von Künstlerpersönlichkeit und geschaffenem Werk zu verstehen, und die Orte der Produktion lassen sich als magische Laboratorien von Idylle und Kampf lesen. „Der Schein trügt. Er ist aber das Solideste, was es gibt. Der Schein ist die Wirklichkeit",[5] heißt es in Montalbáns Geschichte über das Wahrhaftige von Ereignissen und Orten, und hinter jeder bildhaften Wirklichkeit lässt sich eine andere, wahrhaftigere ausmachen. Und dieser ist Elfie Semotan mit ihren intensiven, subtilen und kippenden Fotobildern auf der Spur.

4 **Manuel Vázquez Montalbán,** Das Quartett, übers. von Theres Moser, Berlin 1998

5 **a.a.O., S. 22**

The Breath of the Work

What is immaterial in an artistic concept cannot be congruently captured in a picture. It is its traces and a temporary solidity that can surface in the photo—for an instant. For this single moment the presence of the photographer opens a view onto the artist, onto his works; a breath of the work can be divined. Never does Semotan define the artist as a creative genius or a creatural demiurge. She scans the personality, allows herself latitude for her own interpretation of the subject's mindset, and plumbs the depths behind the person portrayed. Immanent to her photographic vocabulary is the "tilt", the flip-flopping from glamour to absurdity, from affirmative pose to shaky fragility, from effective presence to blurry absence. Her act of illumination calculates how volumes, capacity, mass can be depicted; her narrative style then eliminates these very cognitive parameters. She tells of buoyant models with flowers in their hand, of a female artist tumbling to the ground, of a baby struggling in the painter's arms; she records the musty darkness of a chaotic studio corner, the halted silent film image of a group of objects taking on a life of their own, an abandoned trailer in the metallic inferno of the American desert.

"I am not who I seem to be" is the confession of the protagonist in Manuel Vázquez Montalbán's short novel "Quartet",[4] in which the description of a murder case turns into a phantasmic scenario. The seemingly so clearly drawn, almost sculpturally defined and presented figures tilt towards precariousness as the story progresses. Behind the picture of a person stands something else, an idea, a motive, an intention. Who can see beyond and who can speculate on what is there? The picture of a person always also reveals the picture of what is not shown—and it is just these gaps in the portraits of artists, these in-between places that are significant. To capture this or to incorporate it into photographs is an approach that tells of a scrupulous treatment of person and work and of an ingenious appreciation of both. Elfie Semotan is an artist who photographs artists, sketches them in her own personal hand, outlines, sometimes encompasses them, sometimes only highlights them; the atmosphere she creates in her photo portraits is always to be understood through the link between the artistic personality and the accomplished work, and the production sites can be read as magical laboratories of idyll and struggle. "Semblance deludes. But it's the most solid thing there is. Semblance is reality,"[5] it reads in Montalbán's story of the truthfulness of events and places, and behind every pictorial reality you can make out another, even truer one. And Elfie Semotan is in quest of this truer reality with her intense, subtle and flip-flopping photographs.

4 **Manuel Vázquez Montalbán,** Quartet, 1989 original title: Cuarteto

5 **Loc. cit., p. 22**

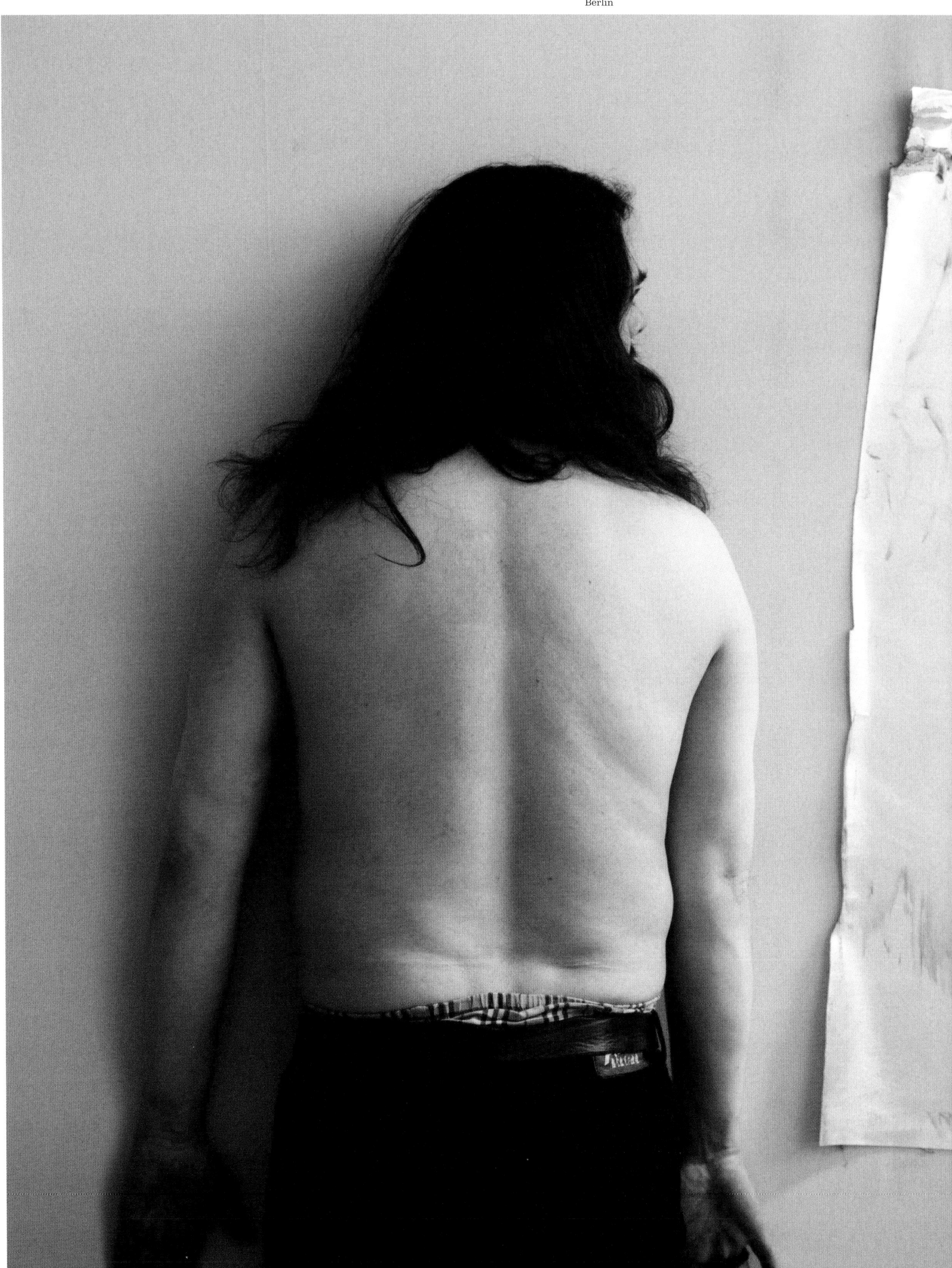

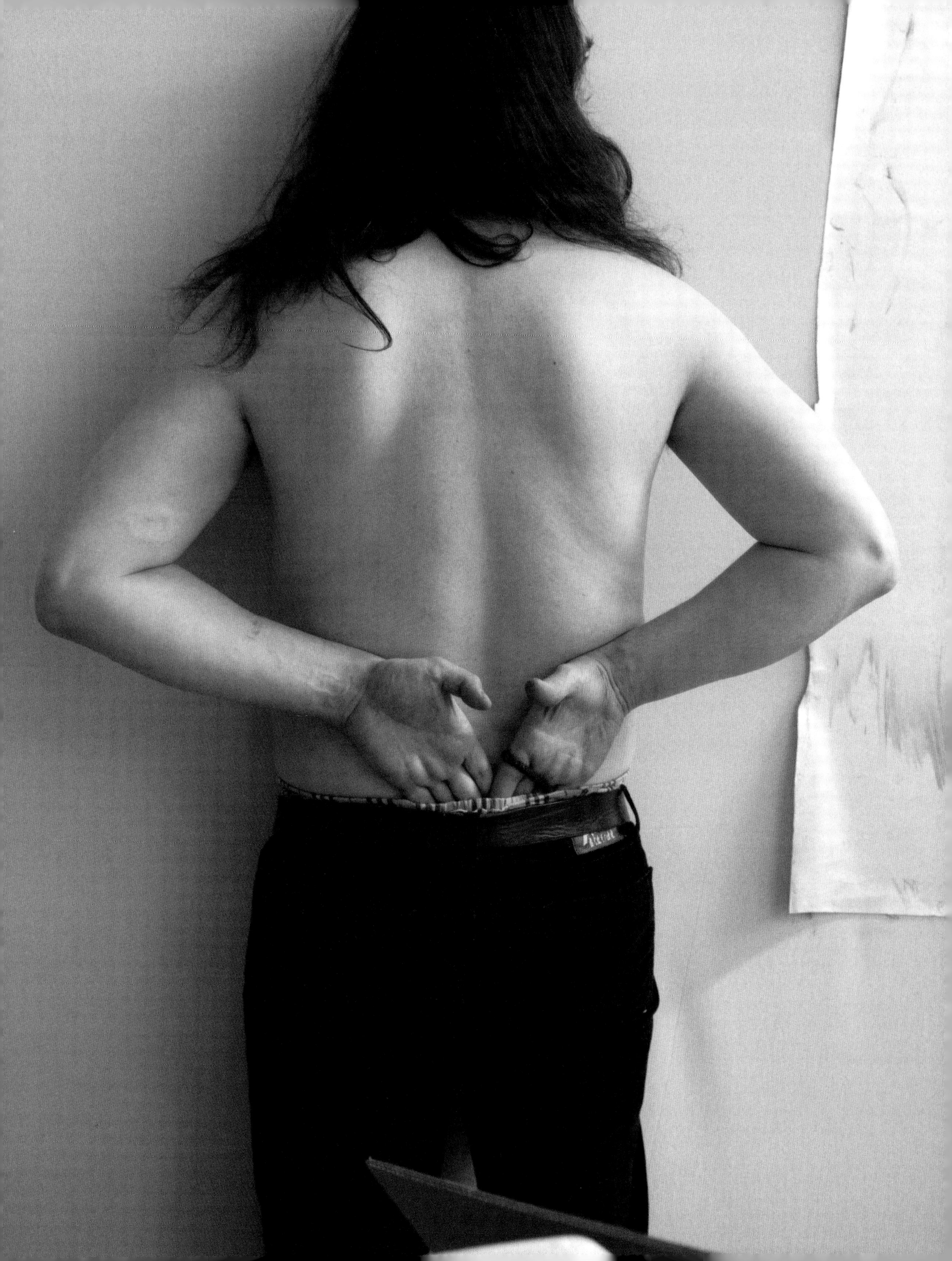

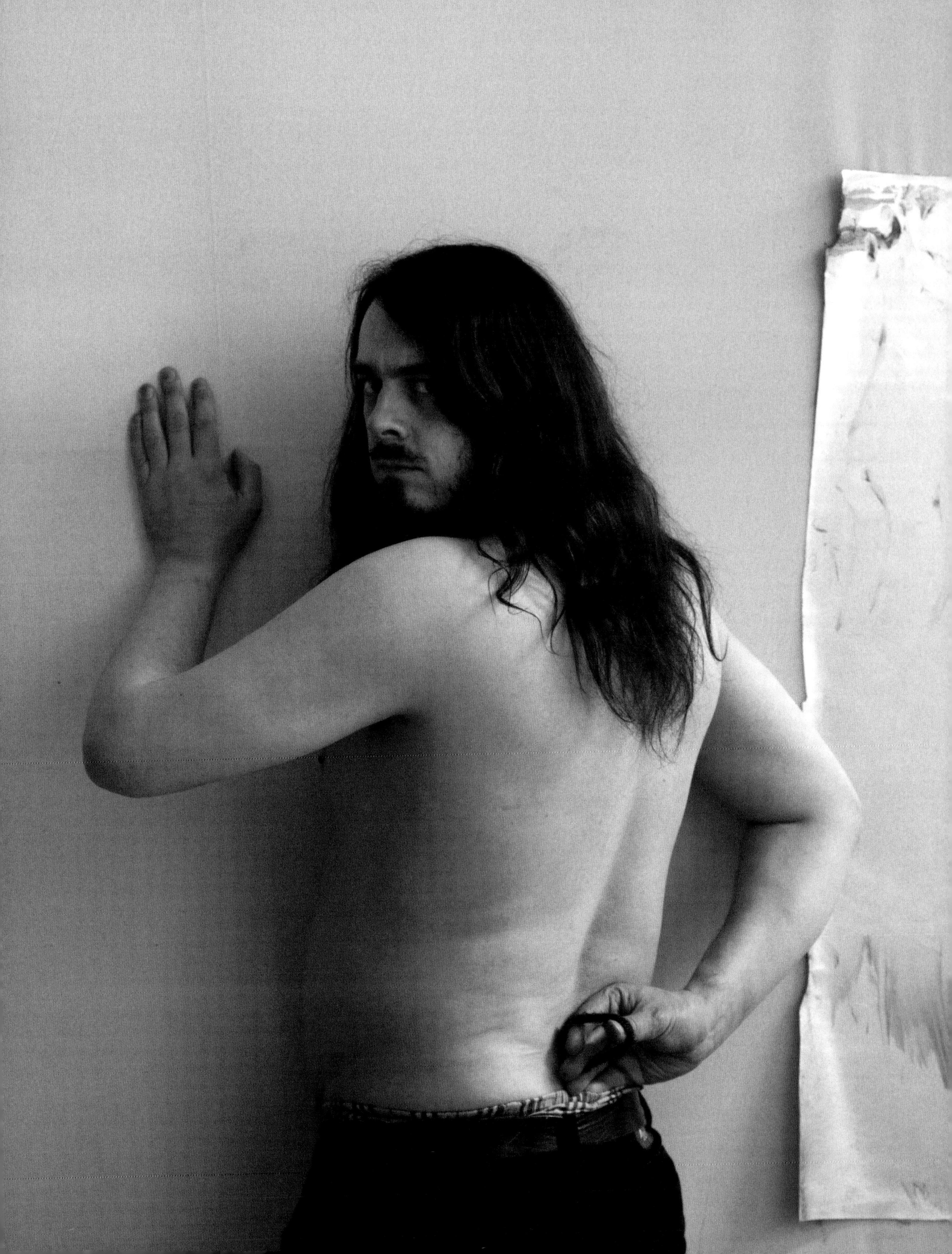

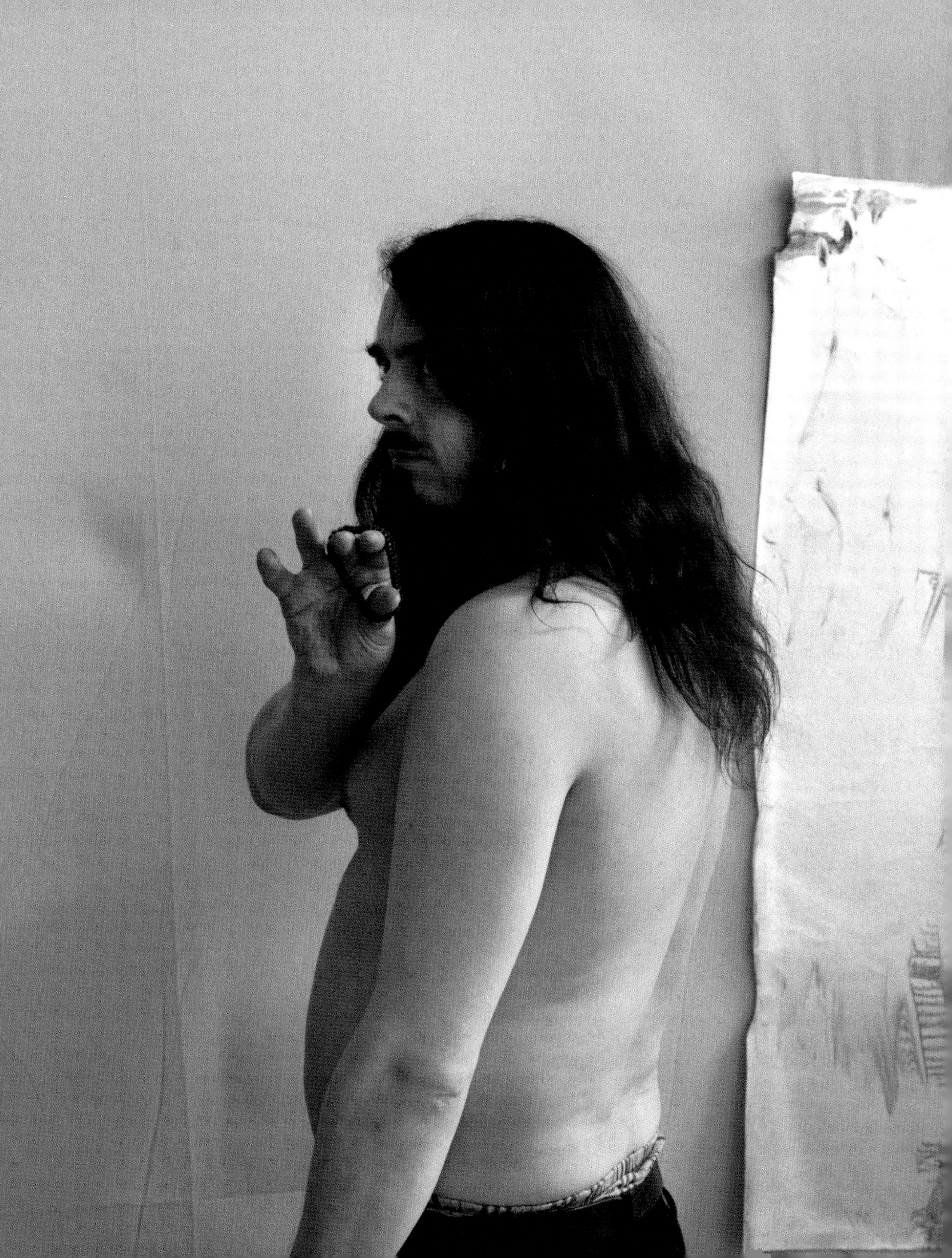

2009 **Georg Baselitz**
Ammersee

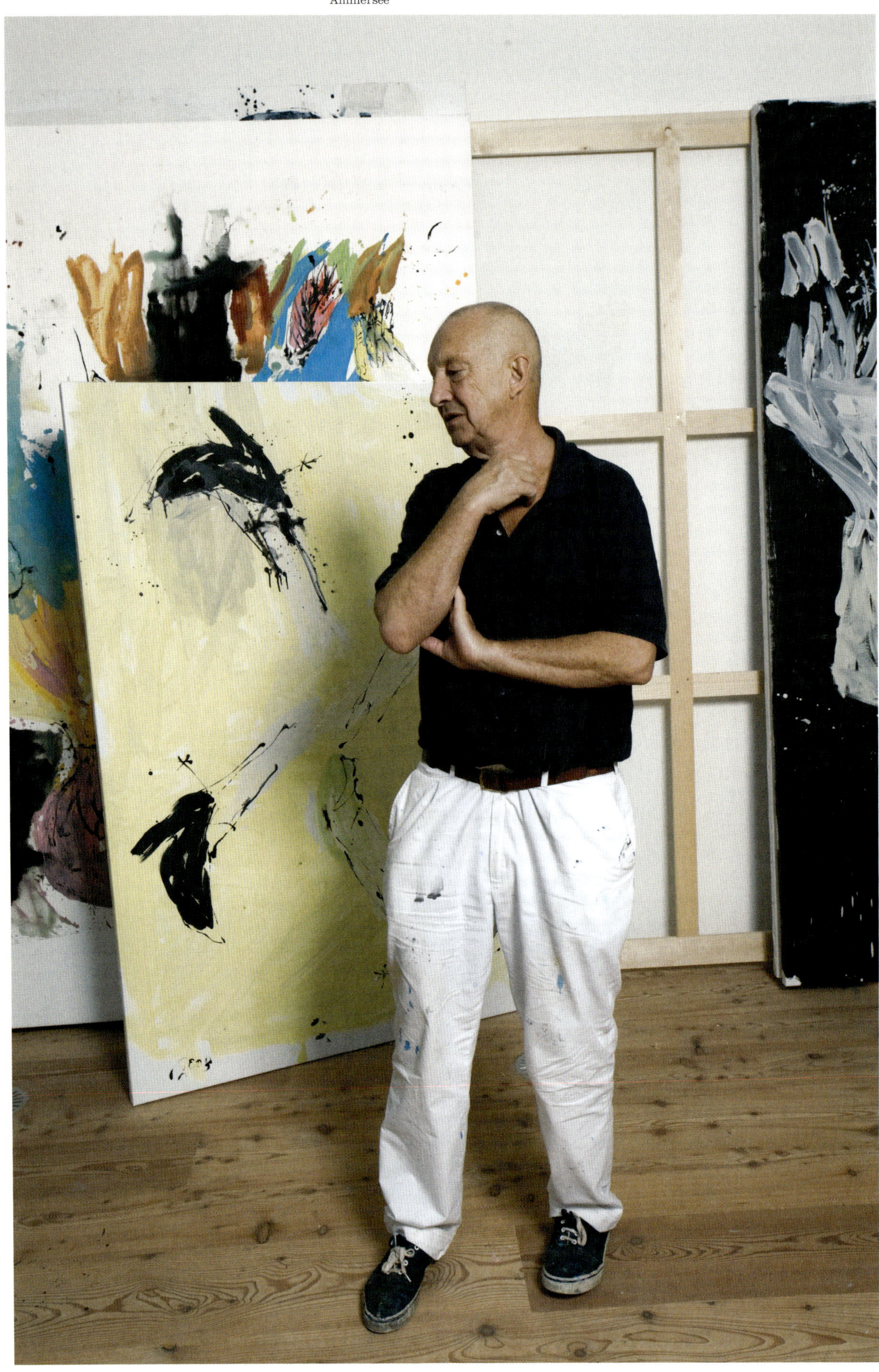

2007 **Angela Bulloch**
Wien/Vienna

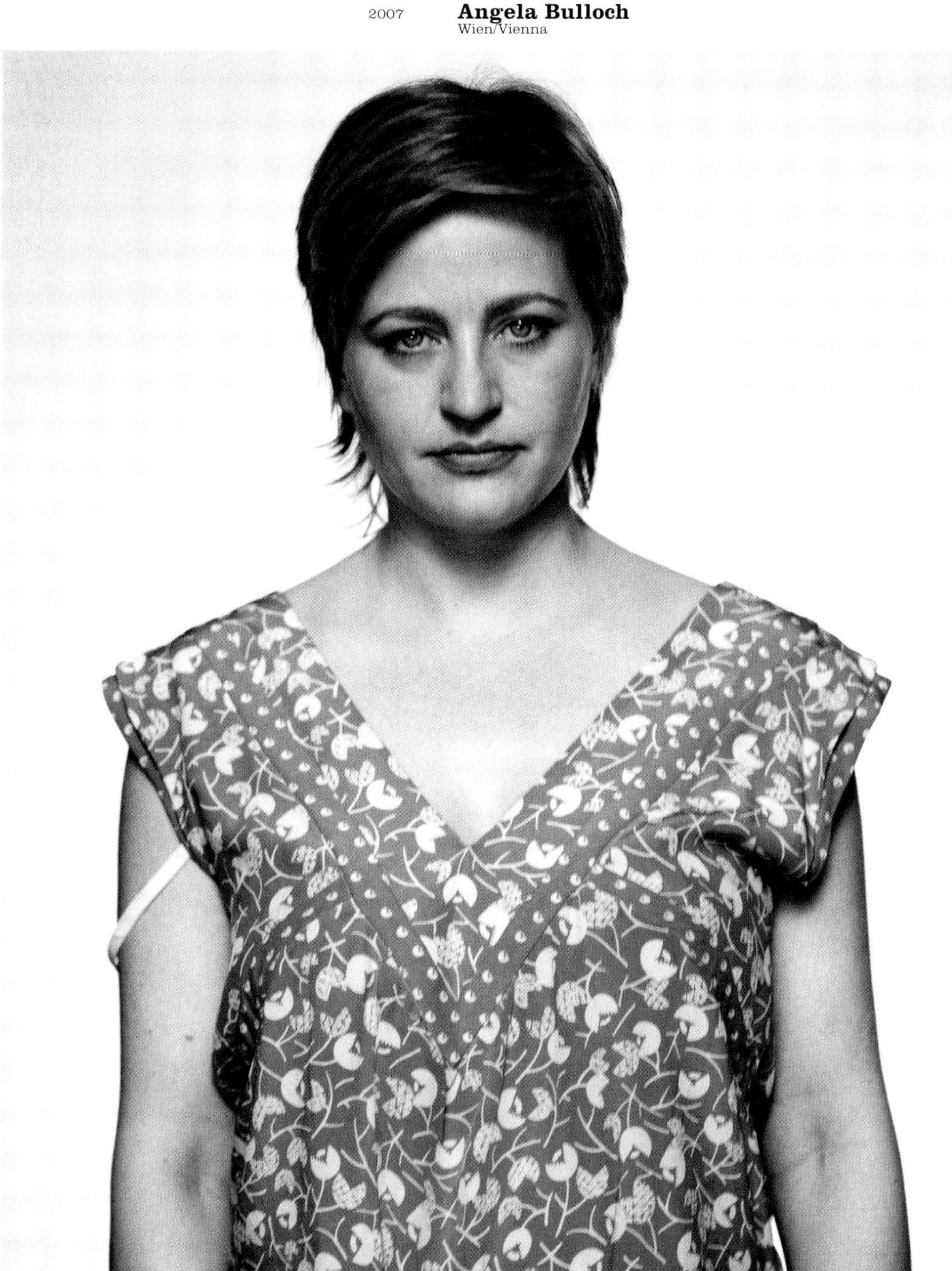

1990 **Otto Zitko Studio**
Wien/Vienna

1990 **Otto Zitko**
Wien/Vienna

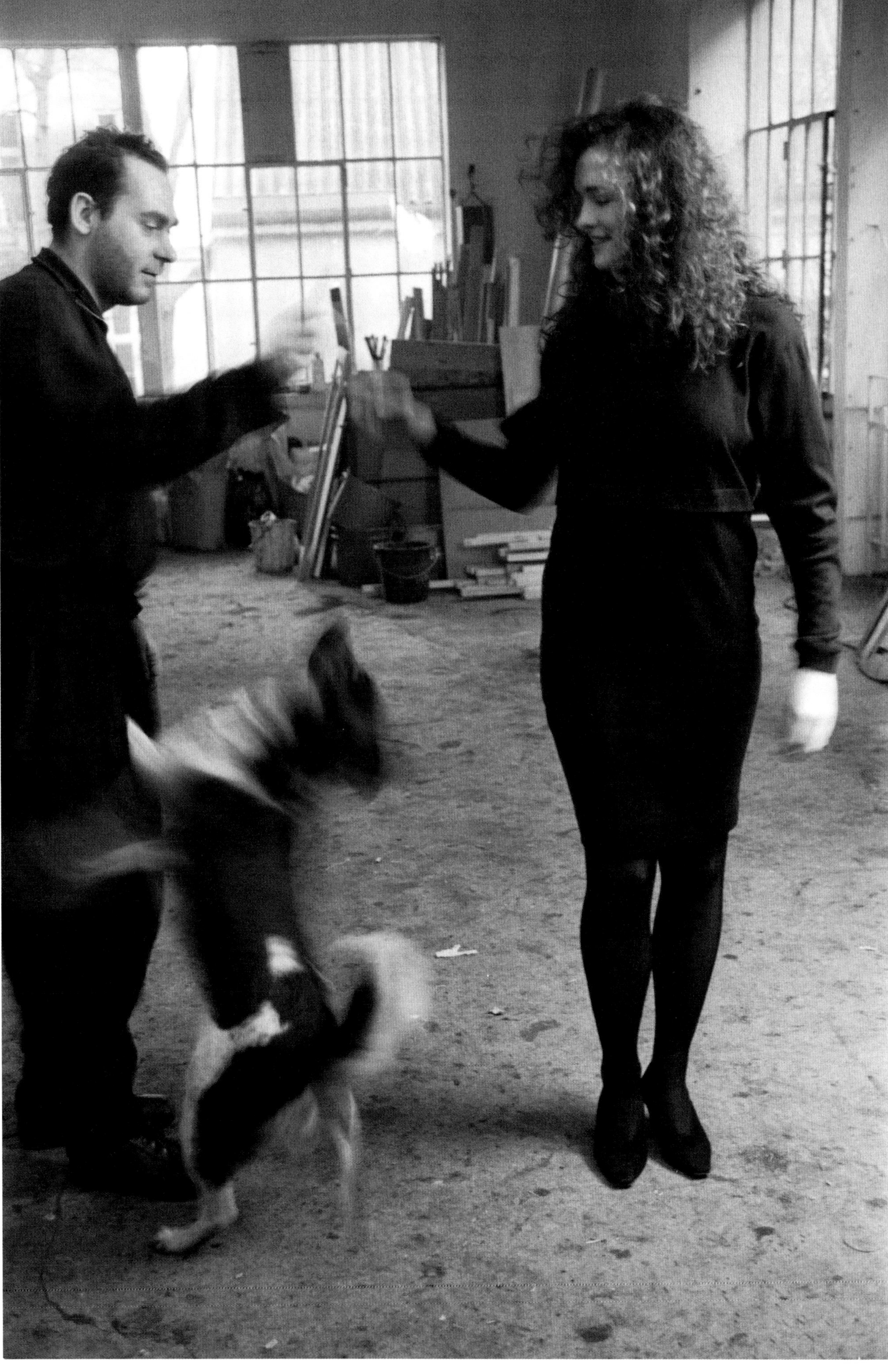

1990 **Otto Zitko Studio**
Wien/Vienna

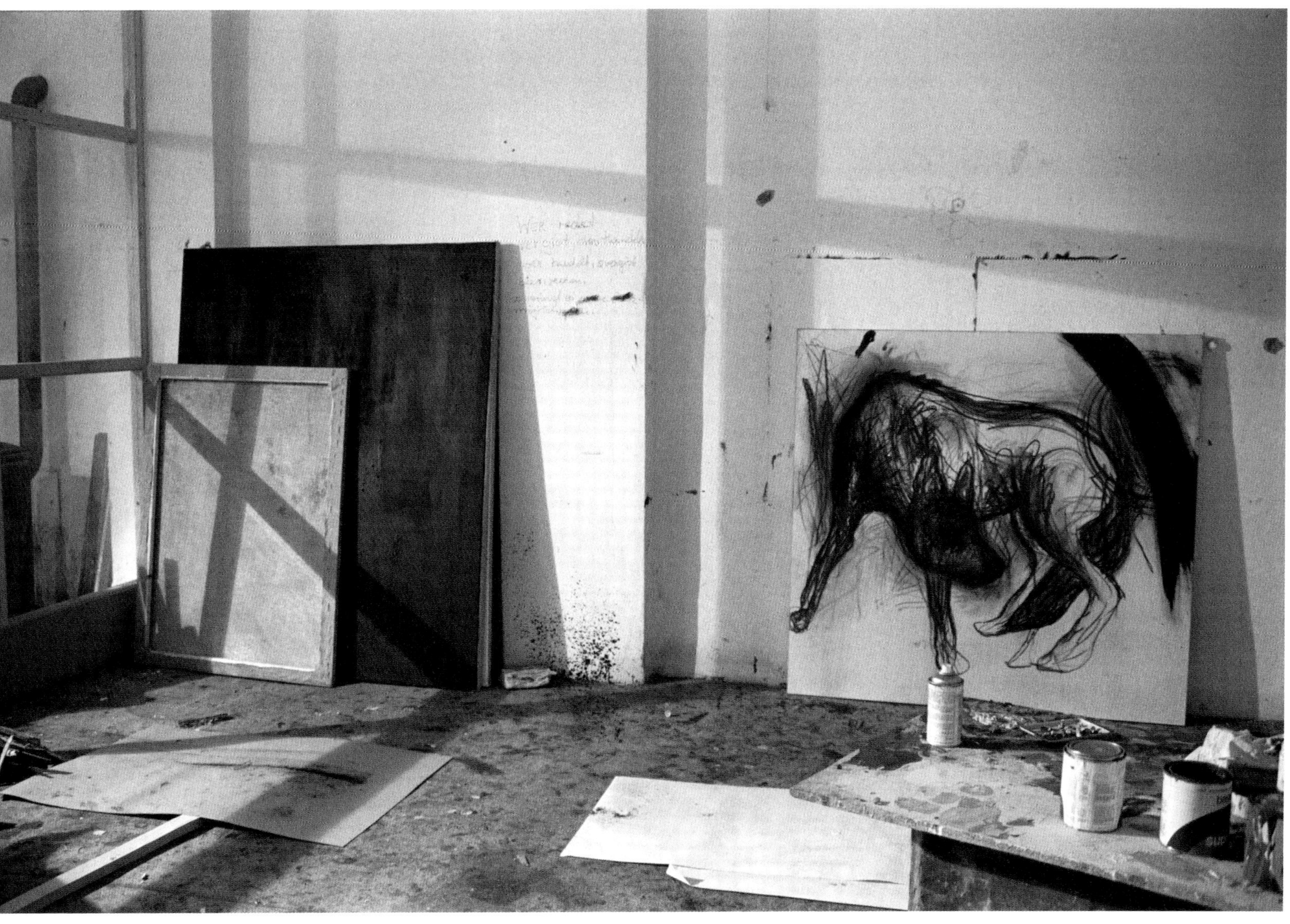

1990 **Walter Obholzer**
Wien/Vienna

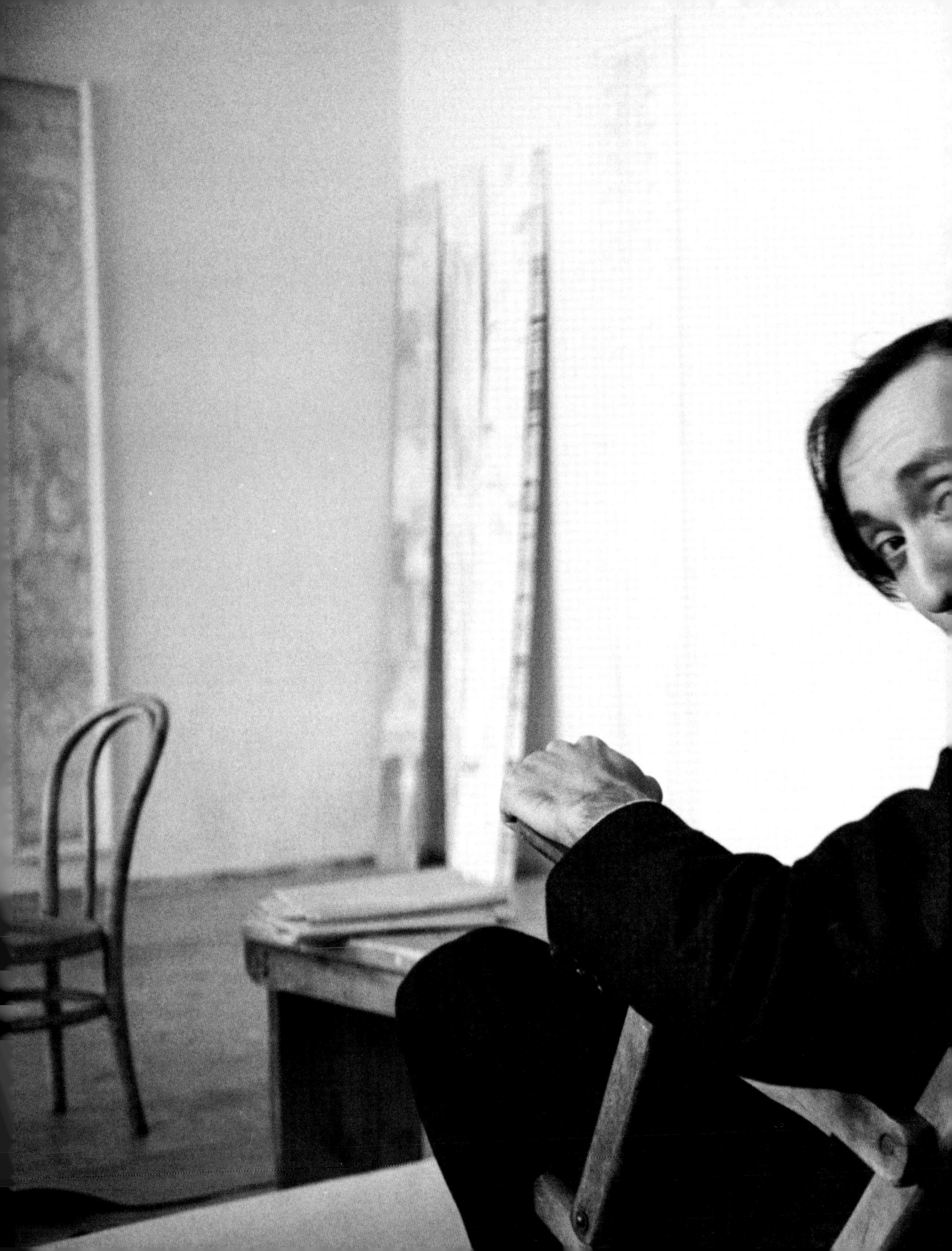

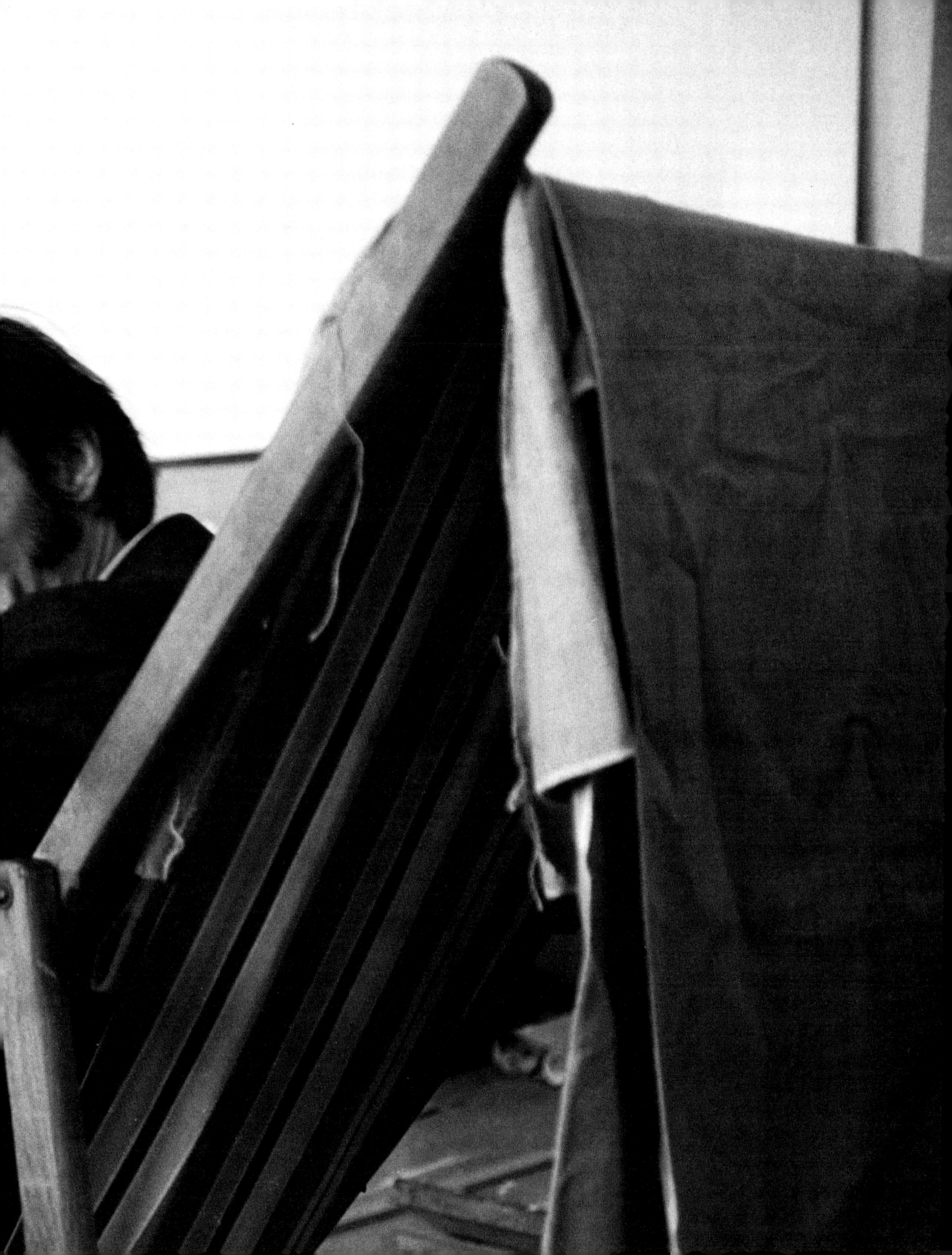

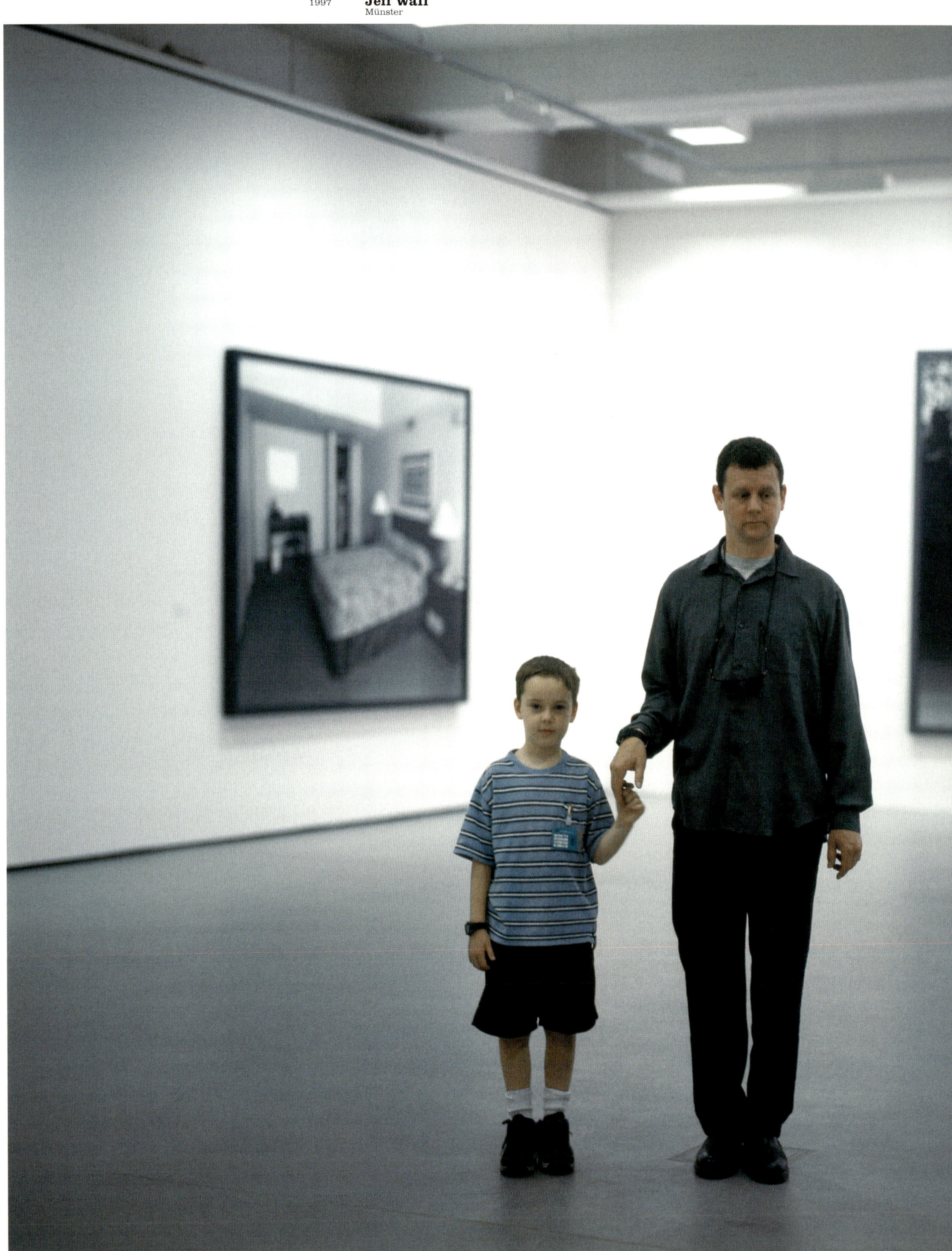

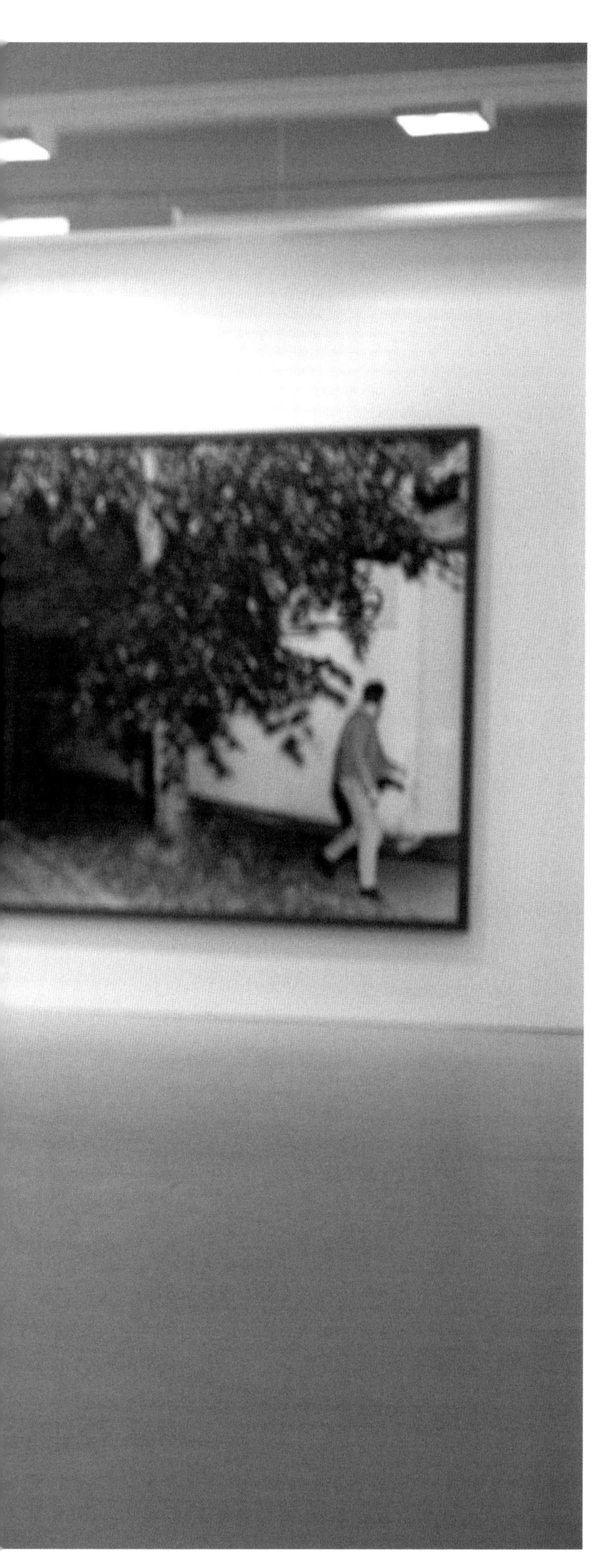

2008 **Daniel Richter Studio**
Berlin

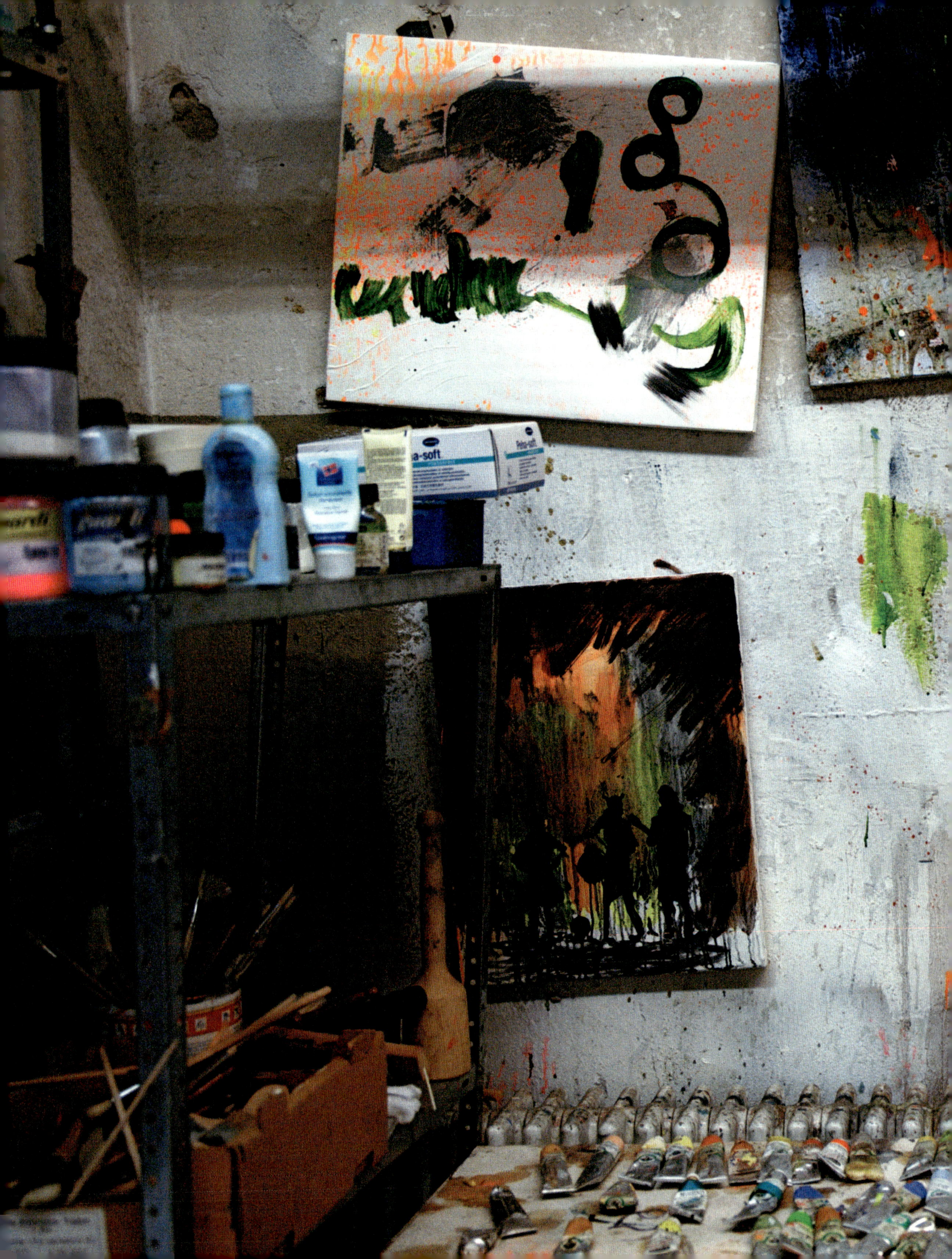

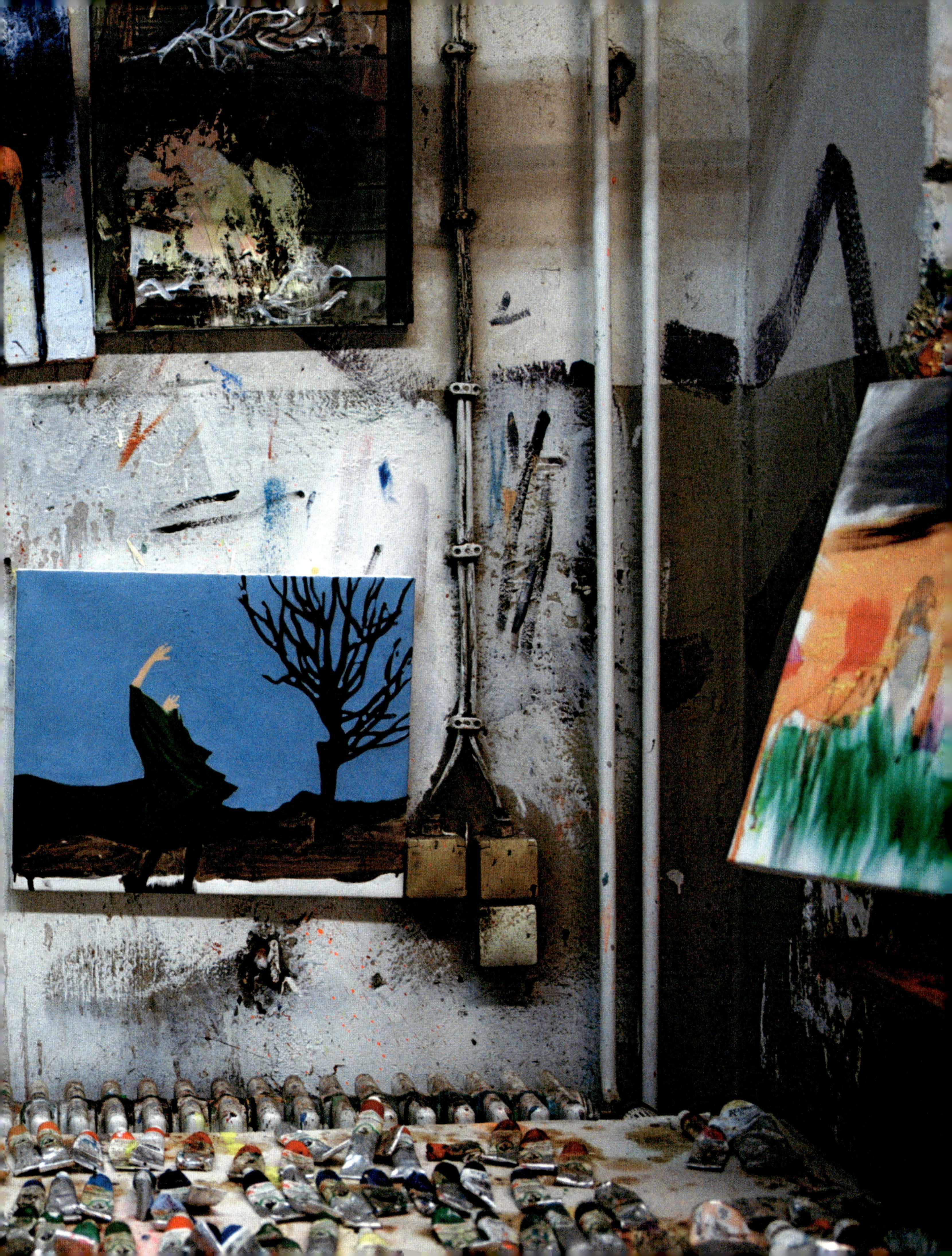

2005 **Katherine Bernhardt**
New York

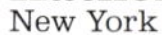

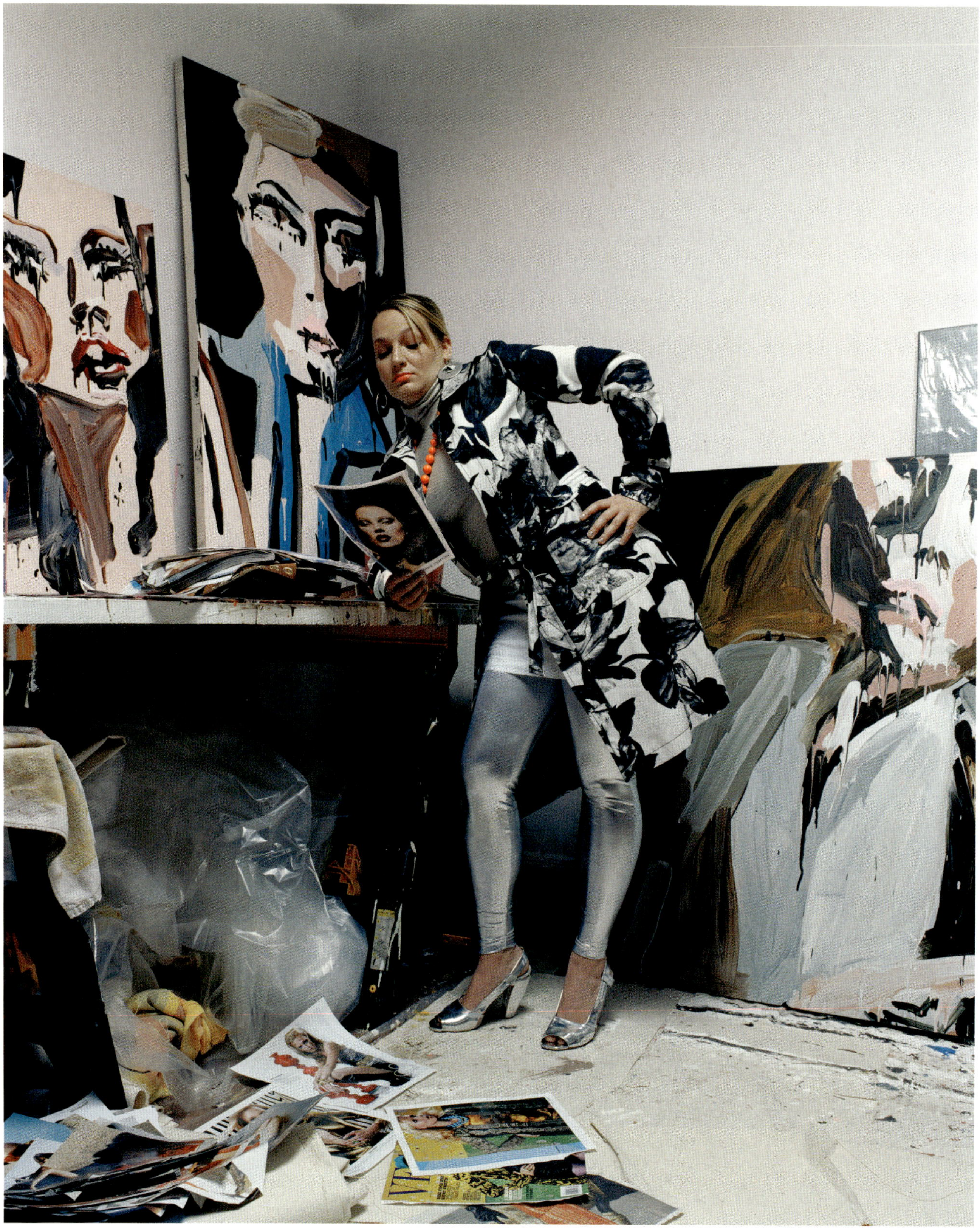

Daniel Richter
Berlin

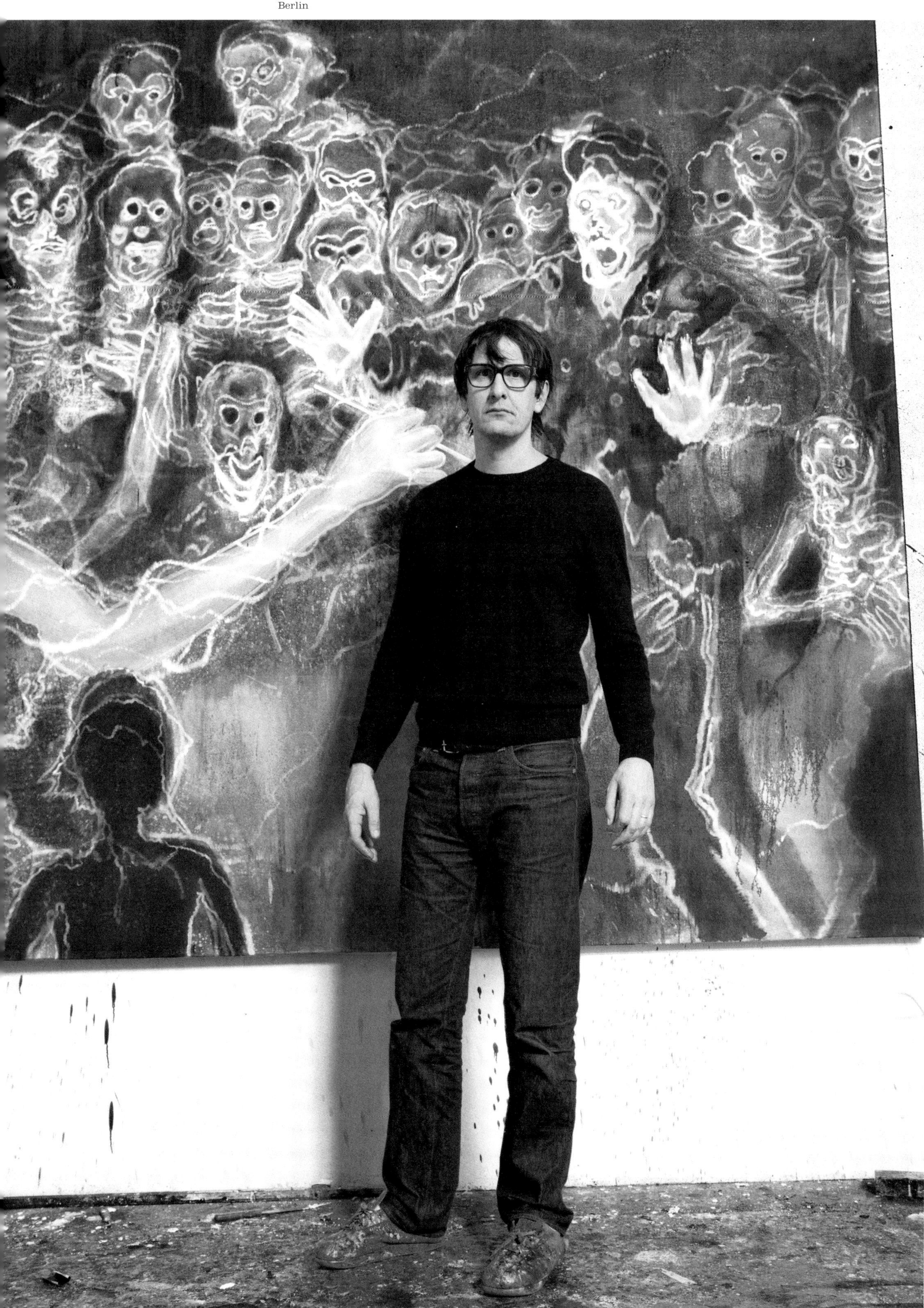

2009 **Dash Snow**
New York

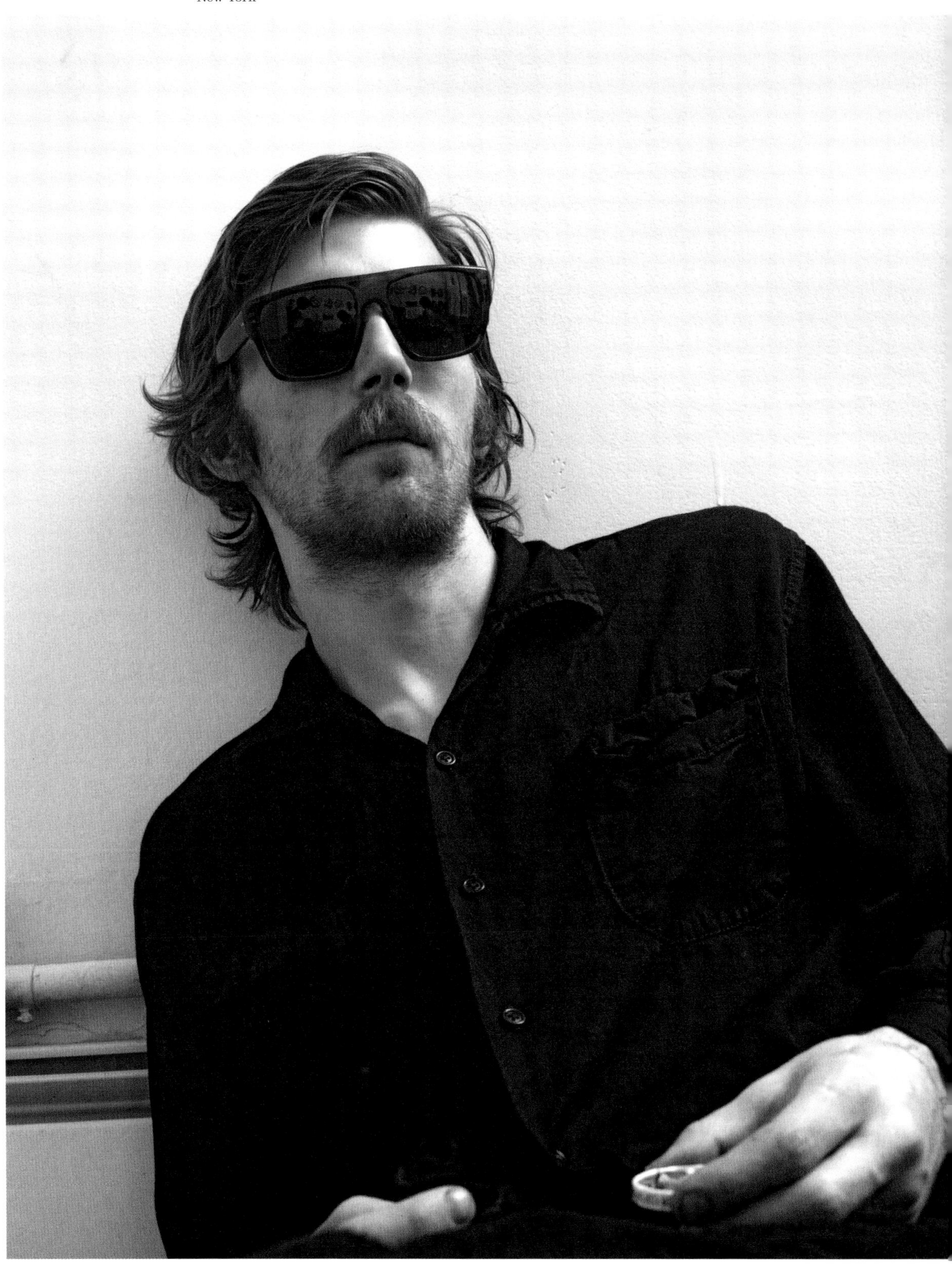

2002 **Alex Katz**
New York

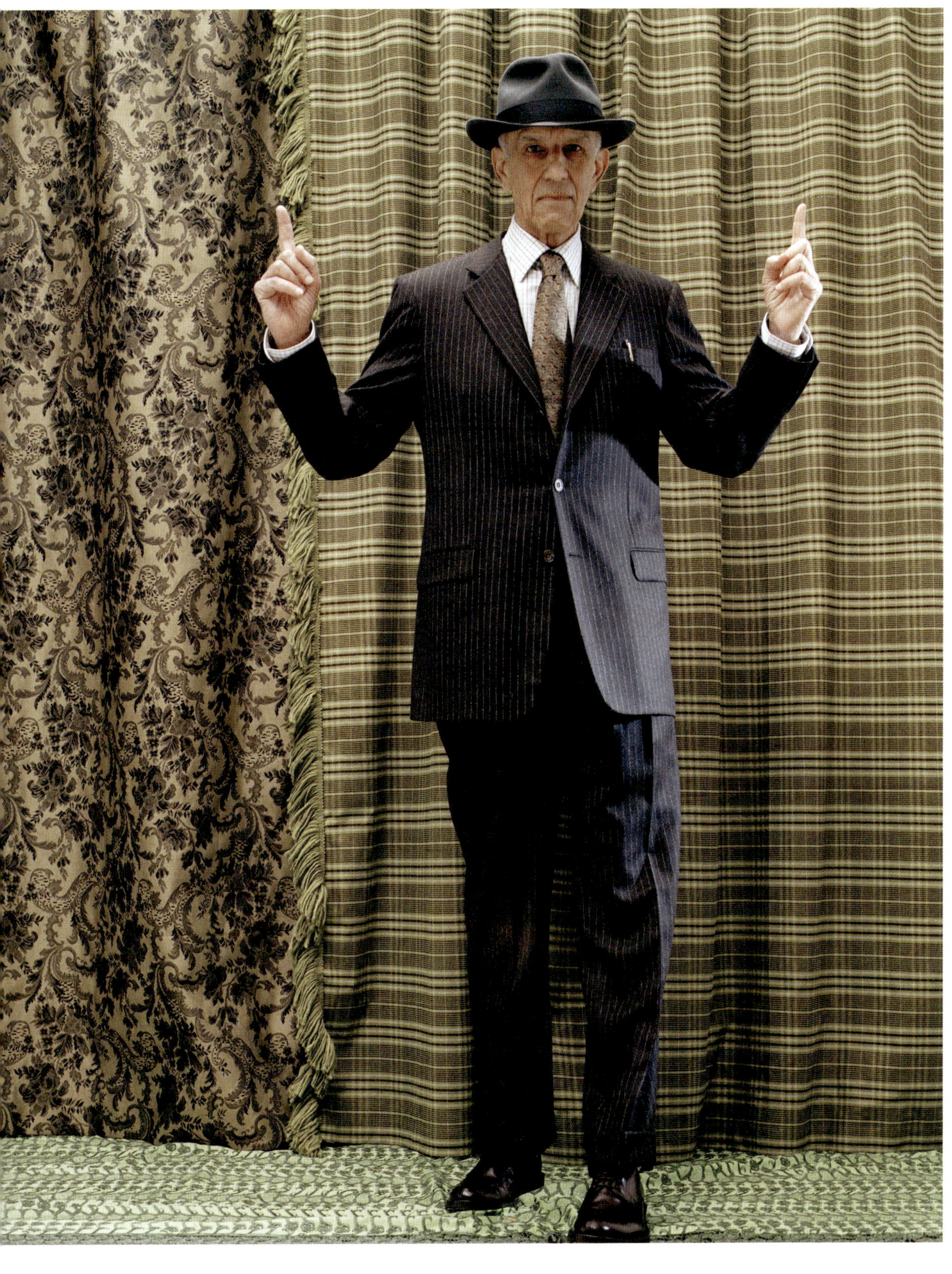

1990 **Franz West**
Wien/Vienna

1990 **Franz West Studio**
Wien/Vienna

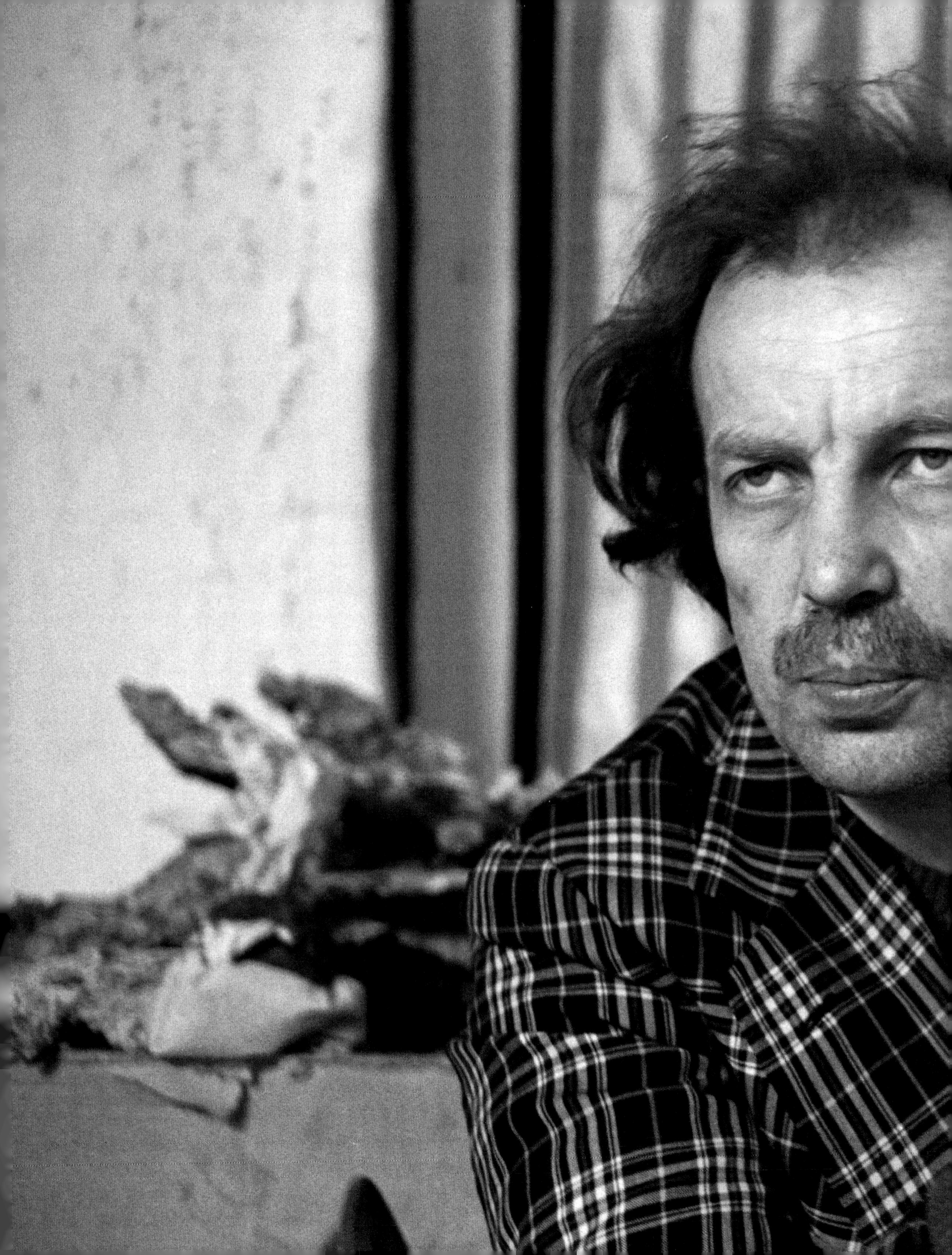

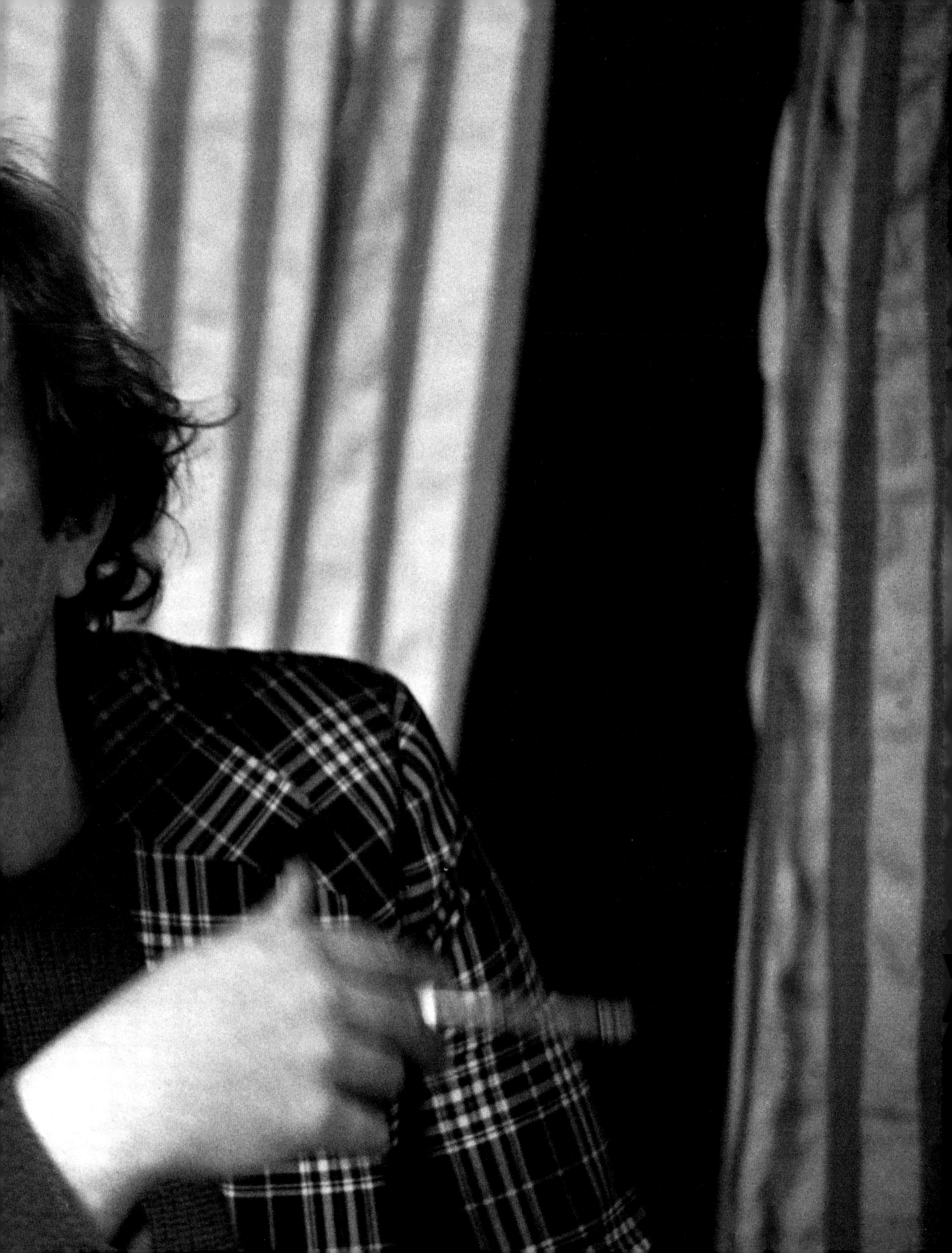

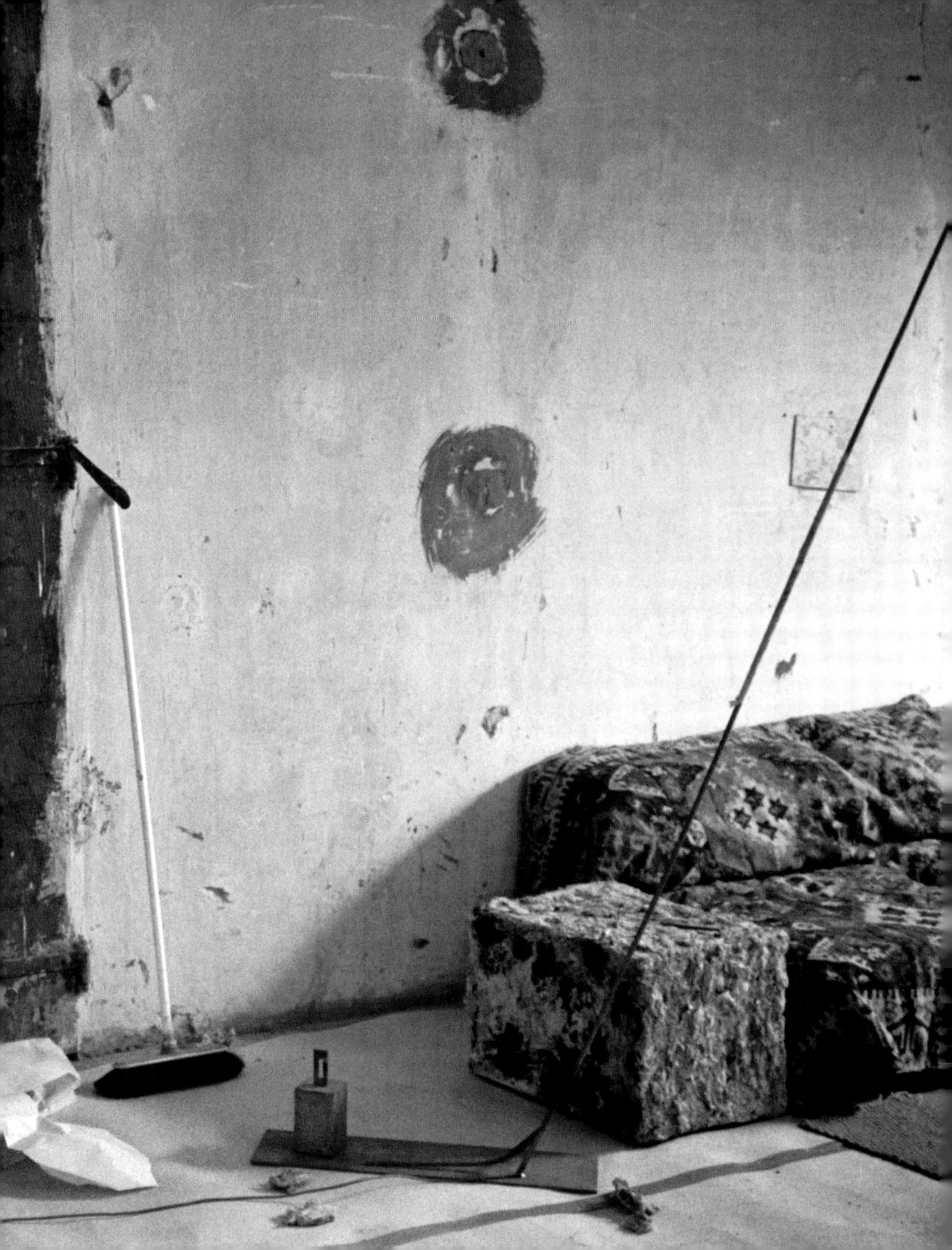

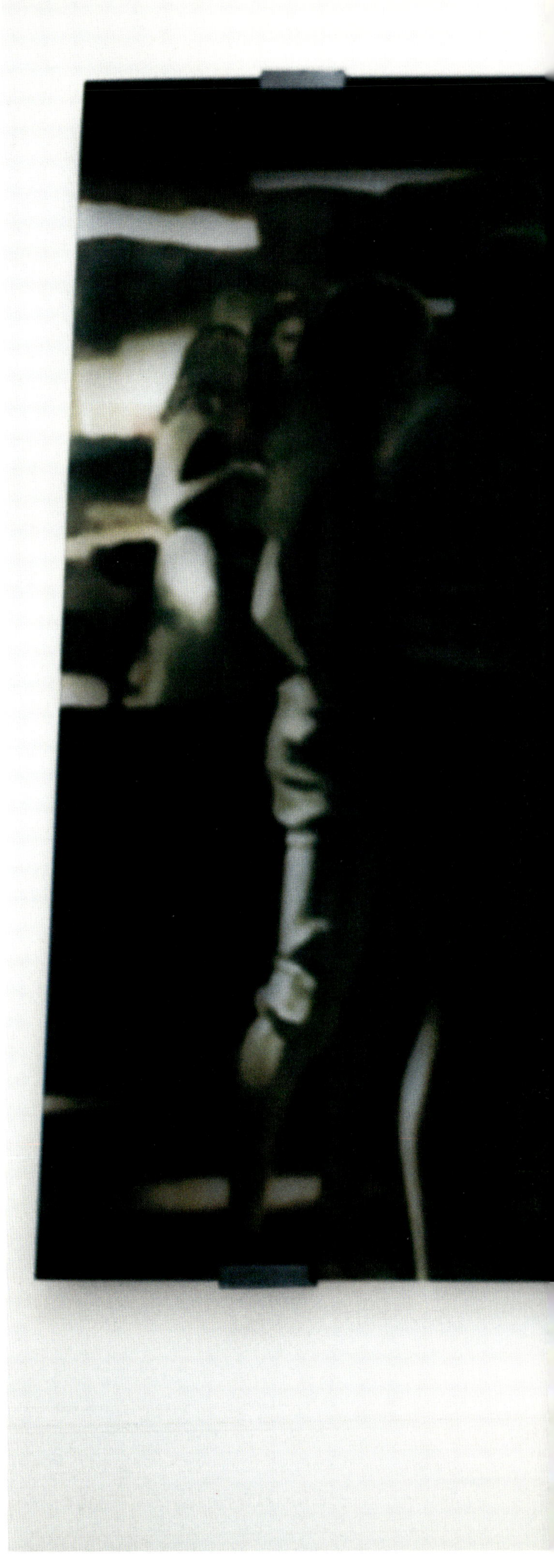

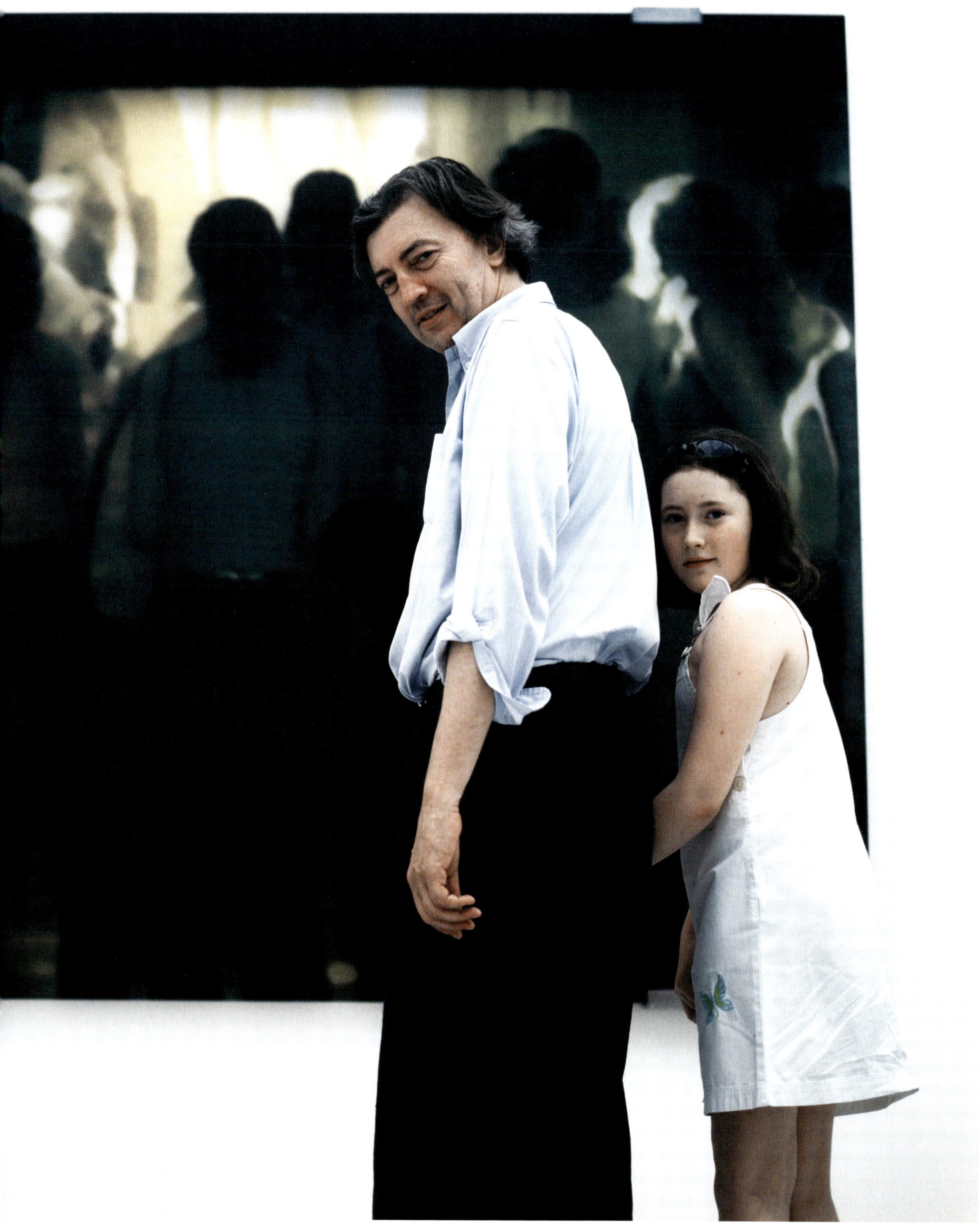

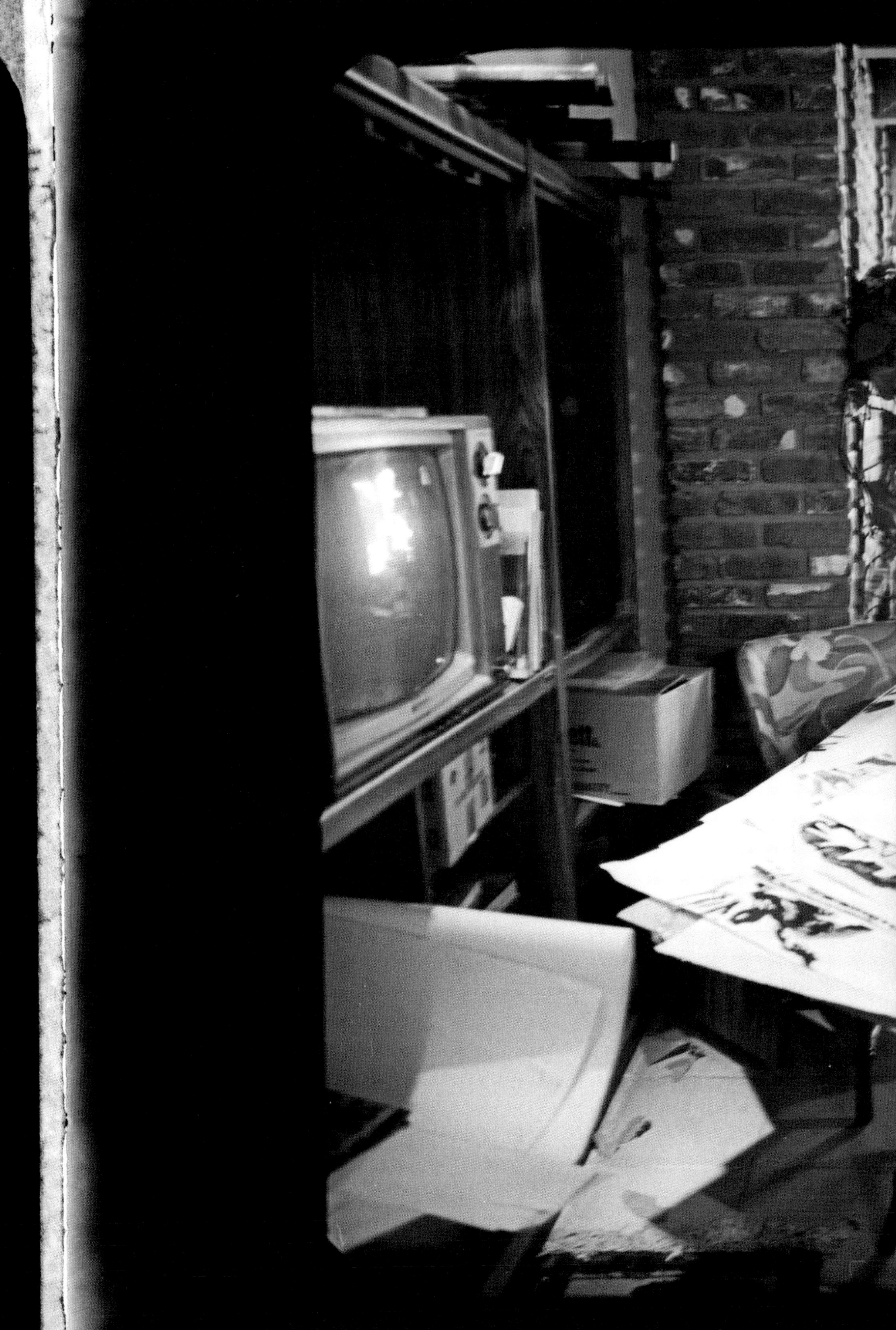

2001 **Raymond Pettibon Studio**
Los Angeles

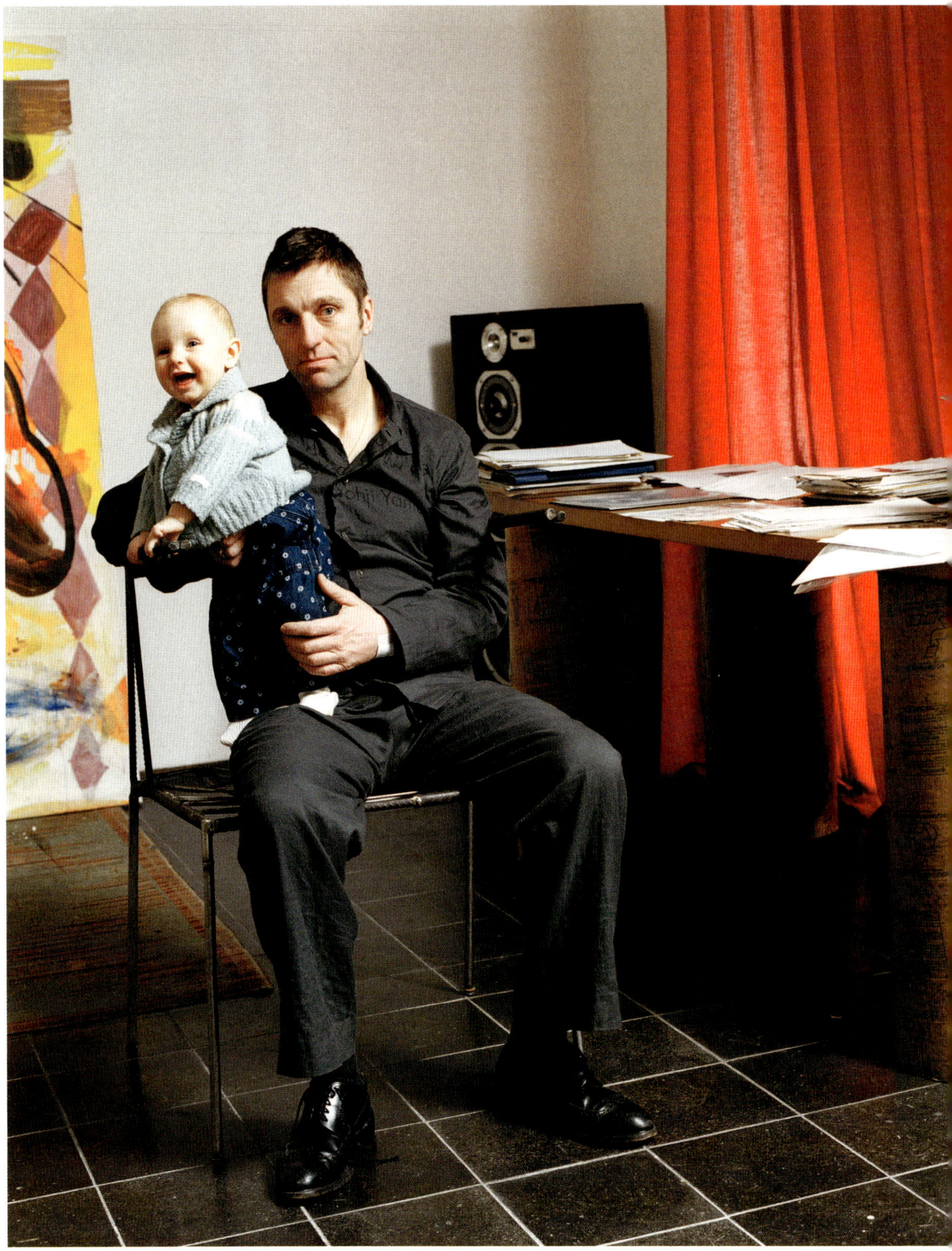

Albert Oehlen
Köln/Cologne

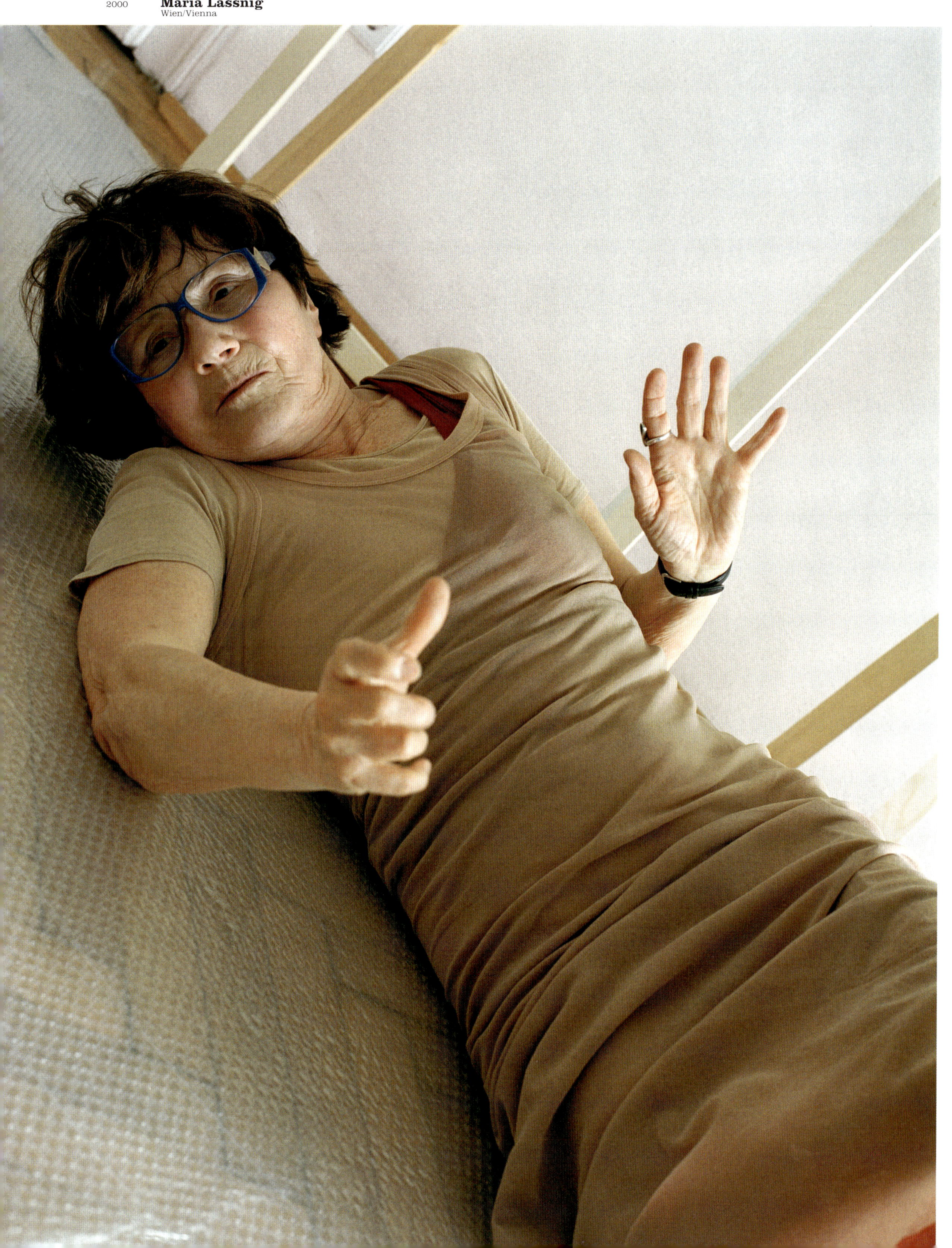

2009

Jake & Dinos Chapman
London

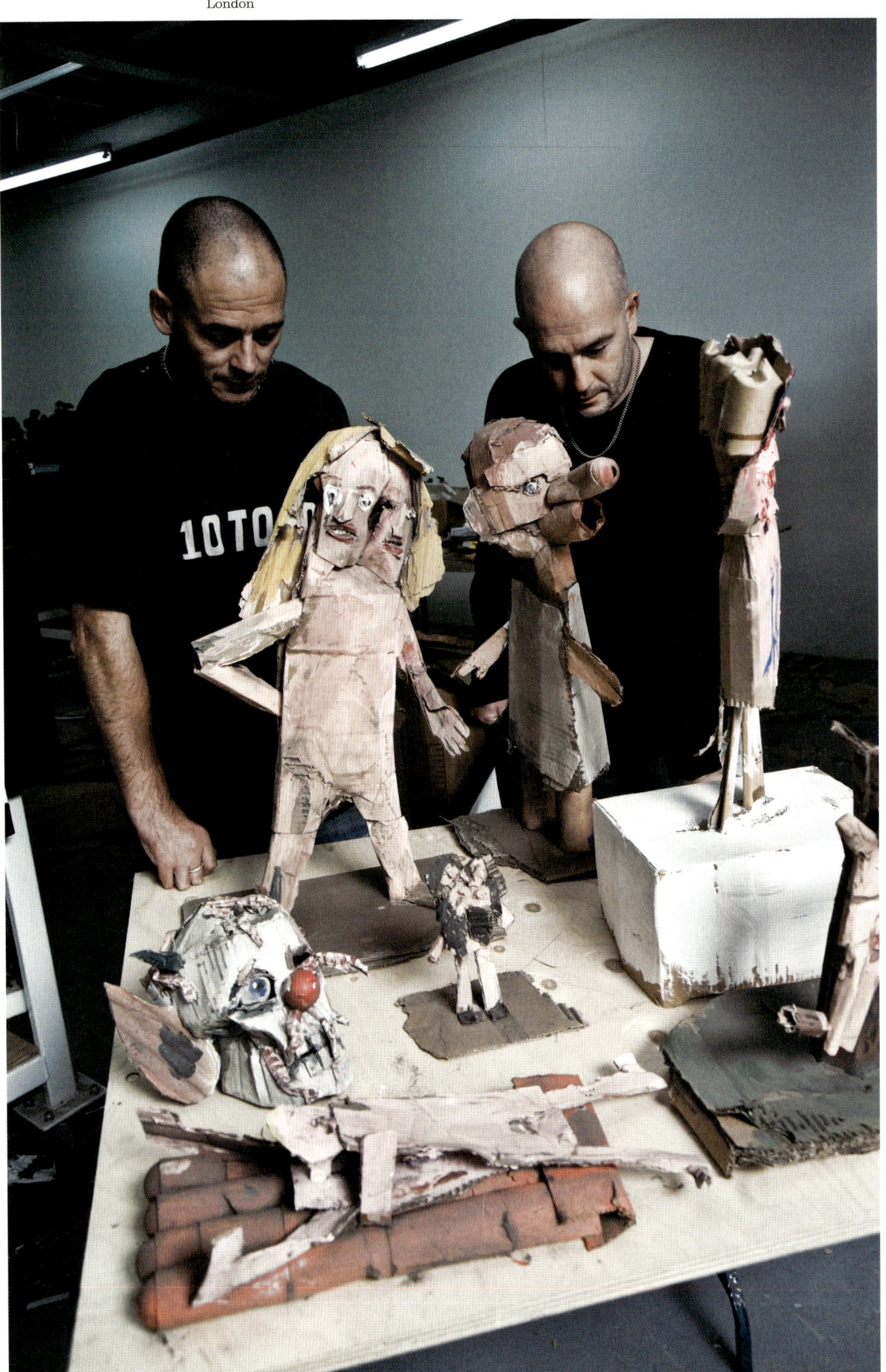

1997 **Lois Weinberger**
Münster

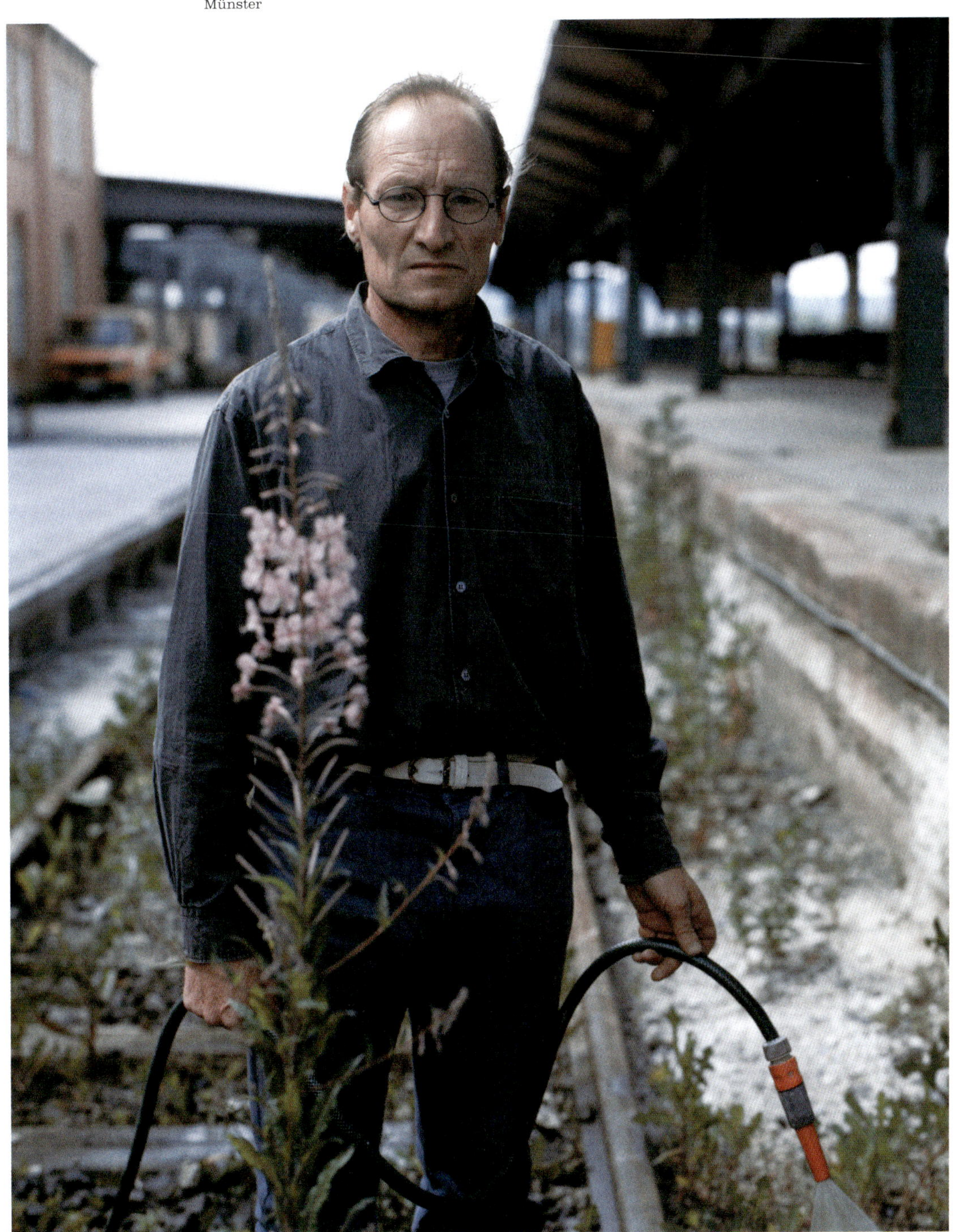

2001 **Raymond Pettibon Studio**
Los Angeles

2001 **Raymond Pettibon**
Los Angeles

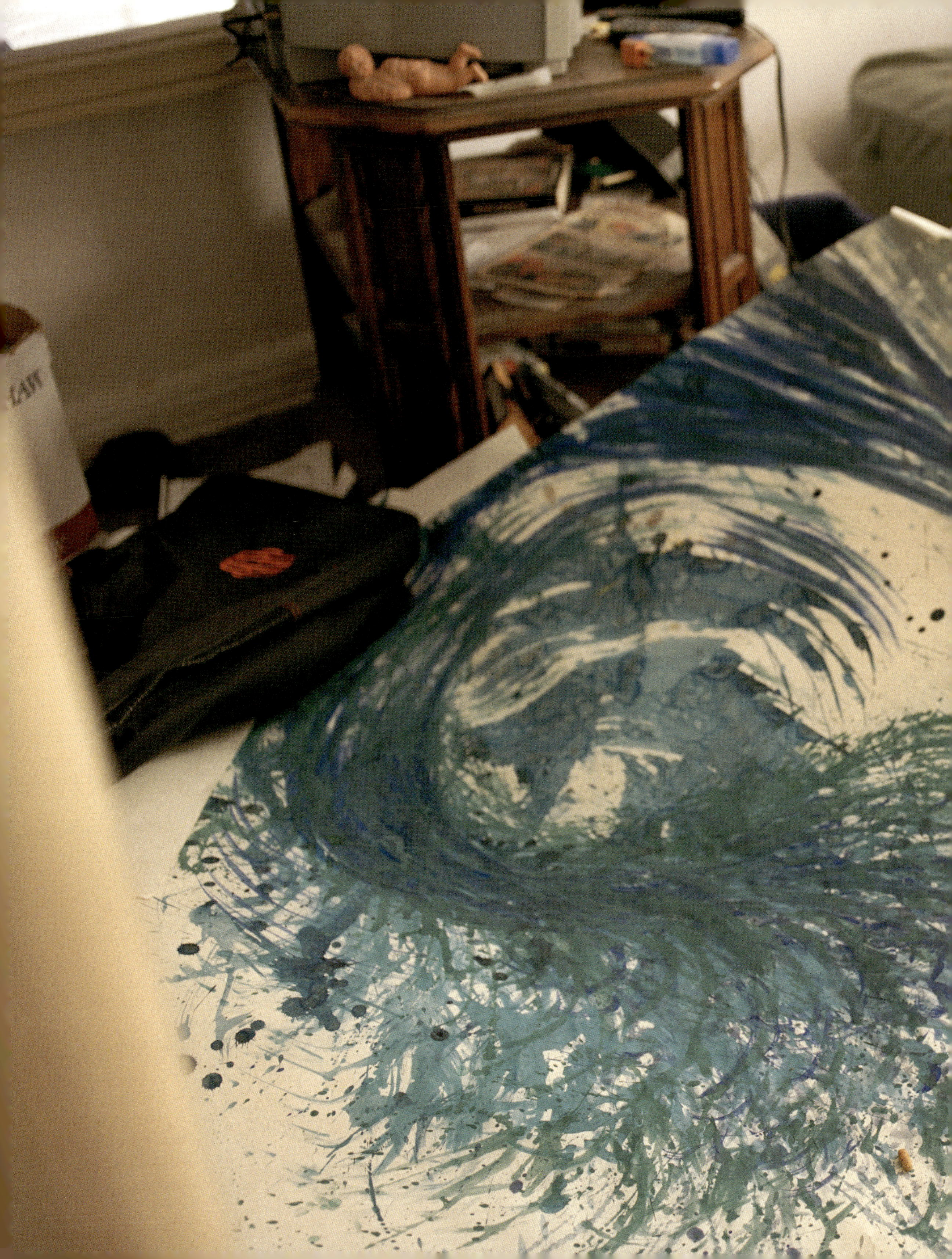

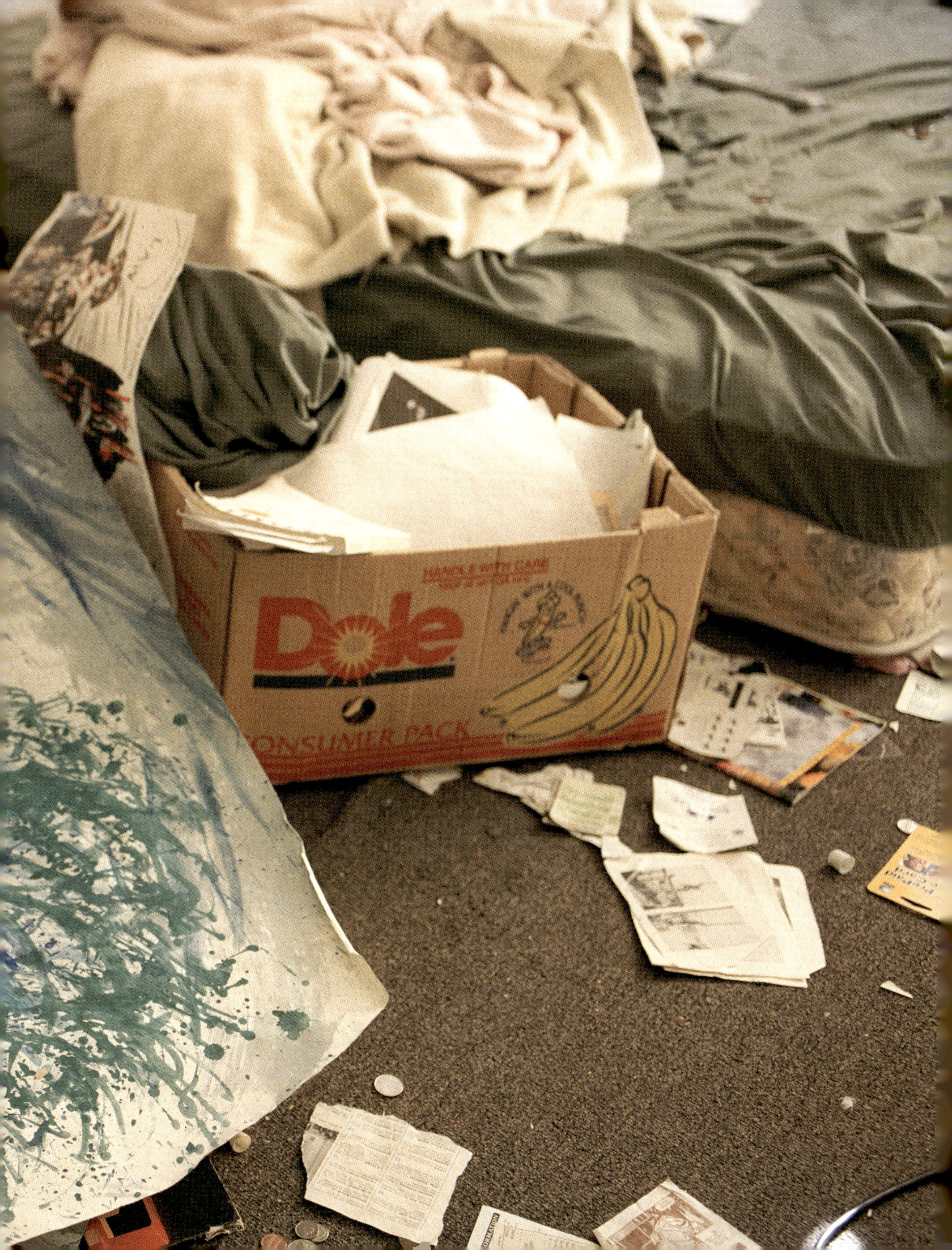
HANDLE WITH CARE
Dole
ONSUMER PACK

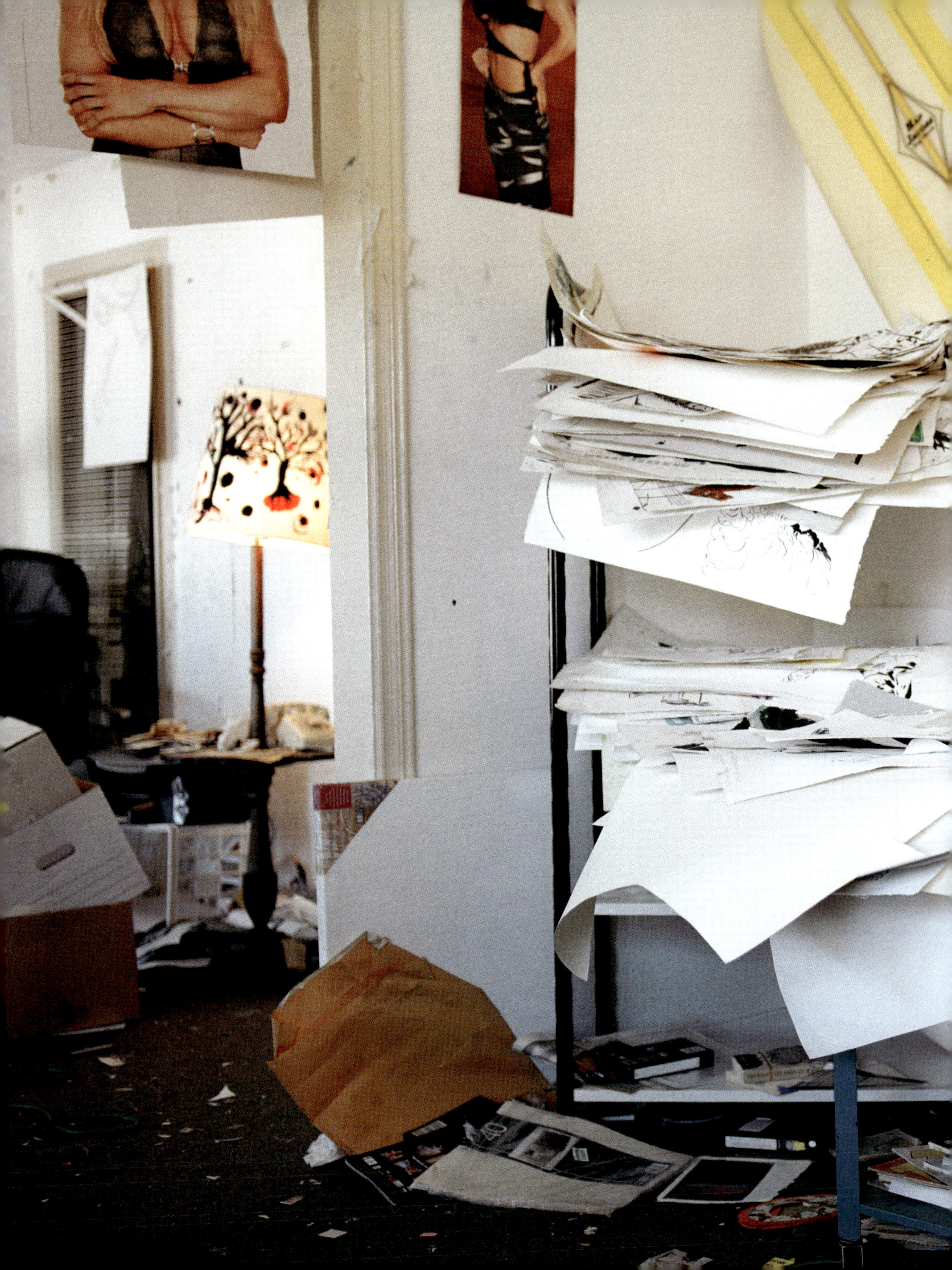

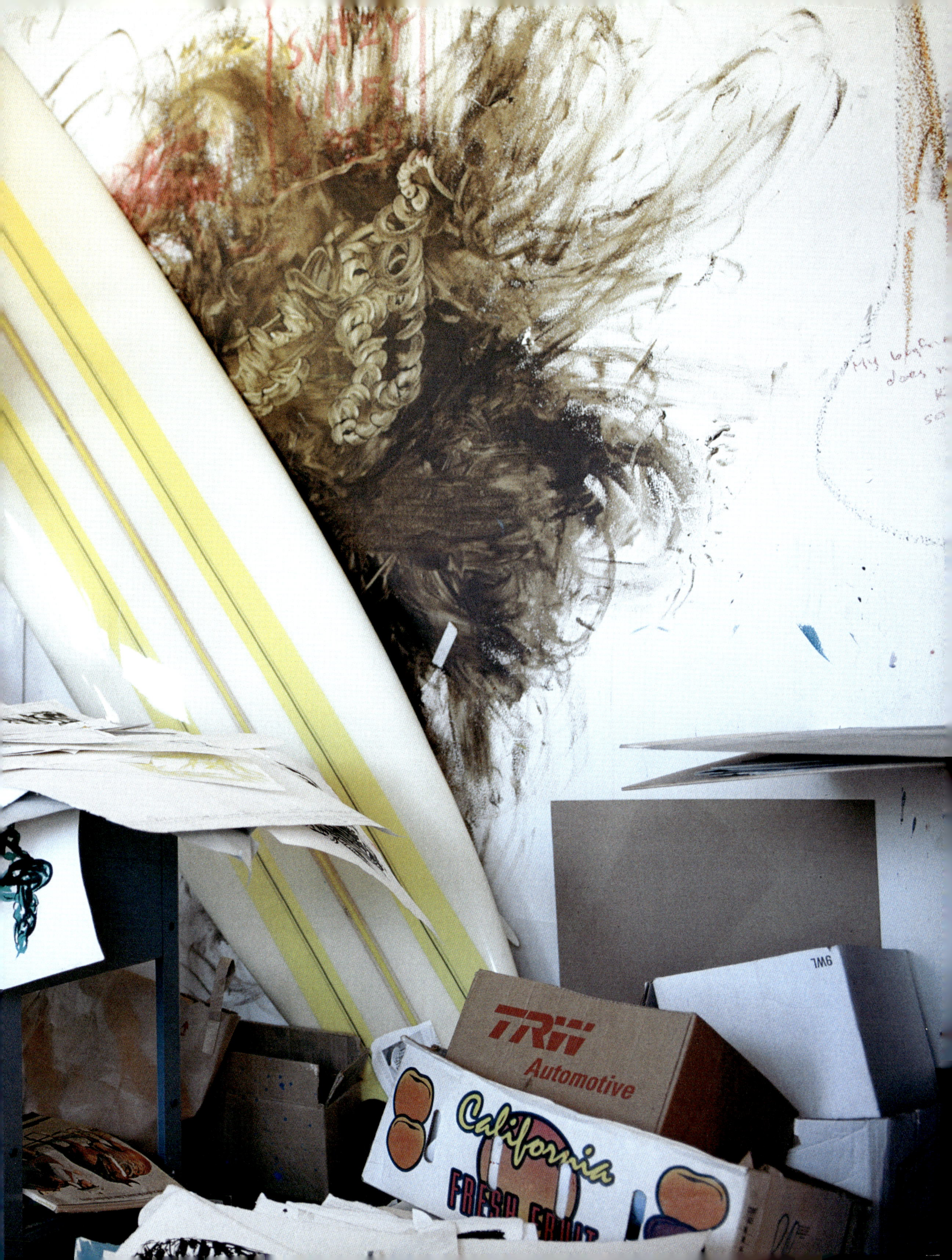

TRW
Automotive
California
FRESH

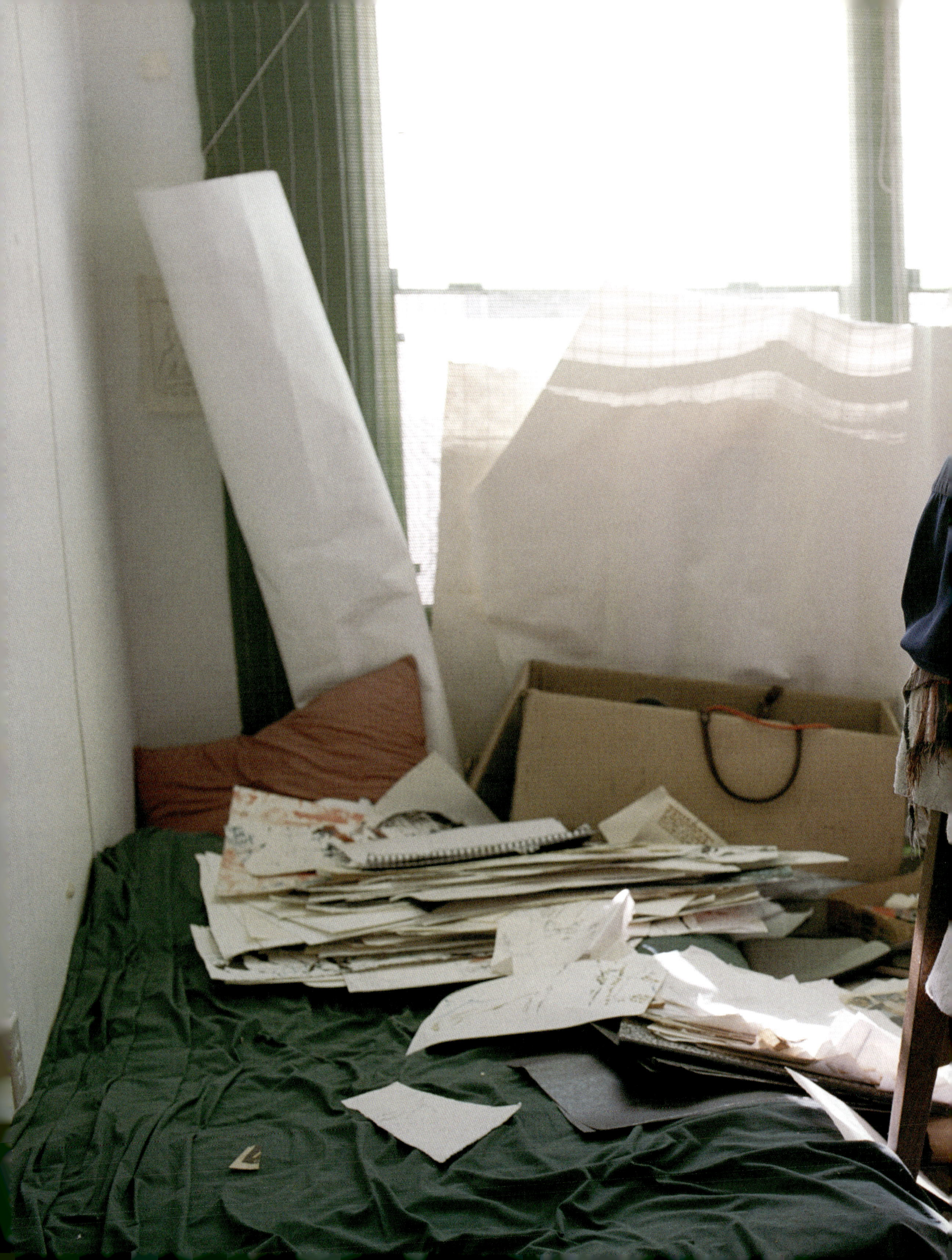

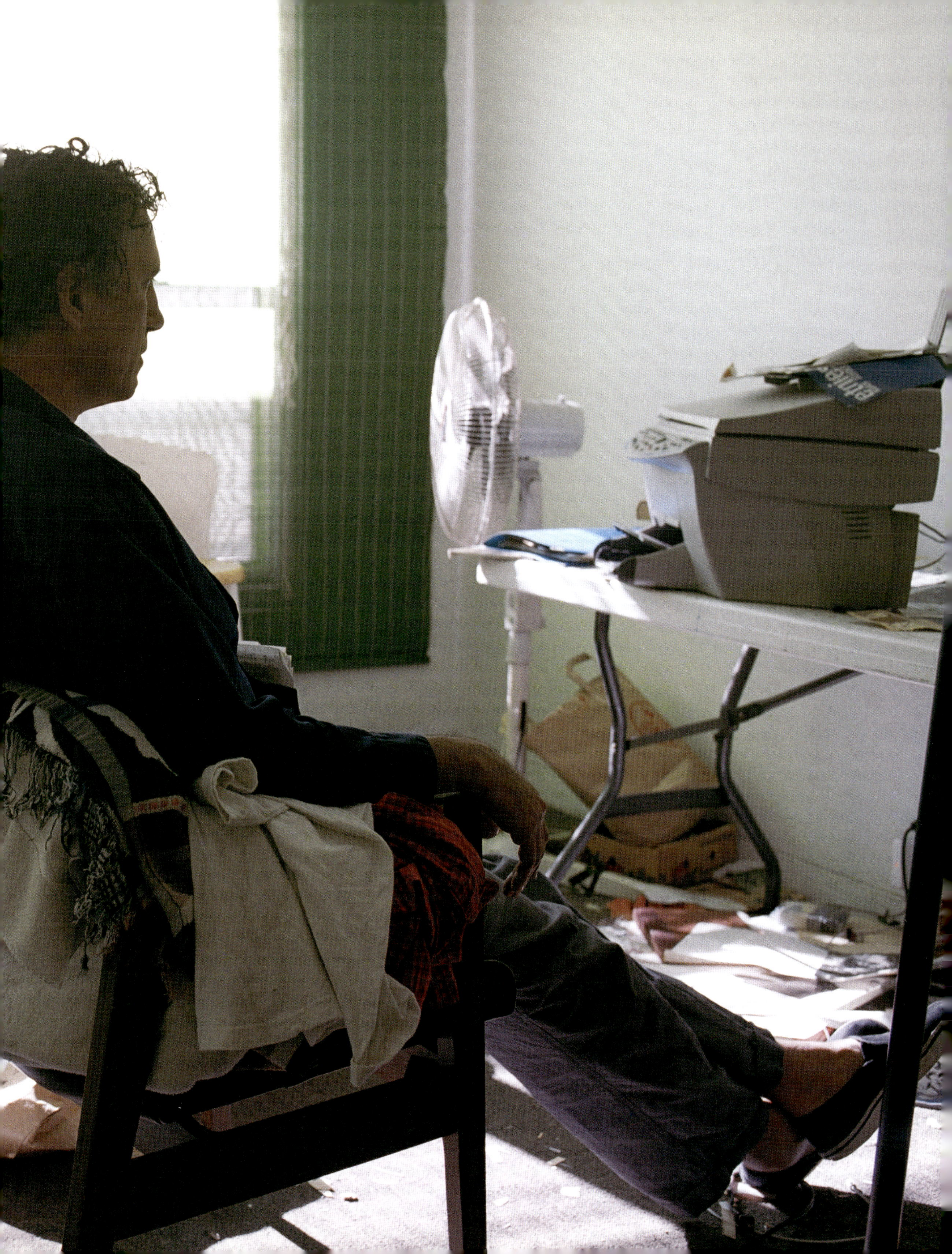

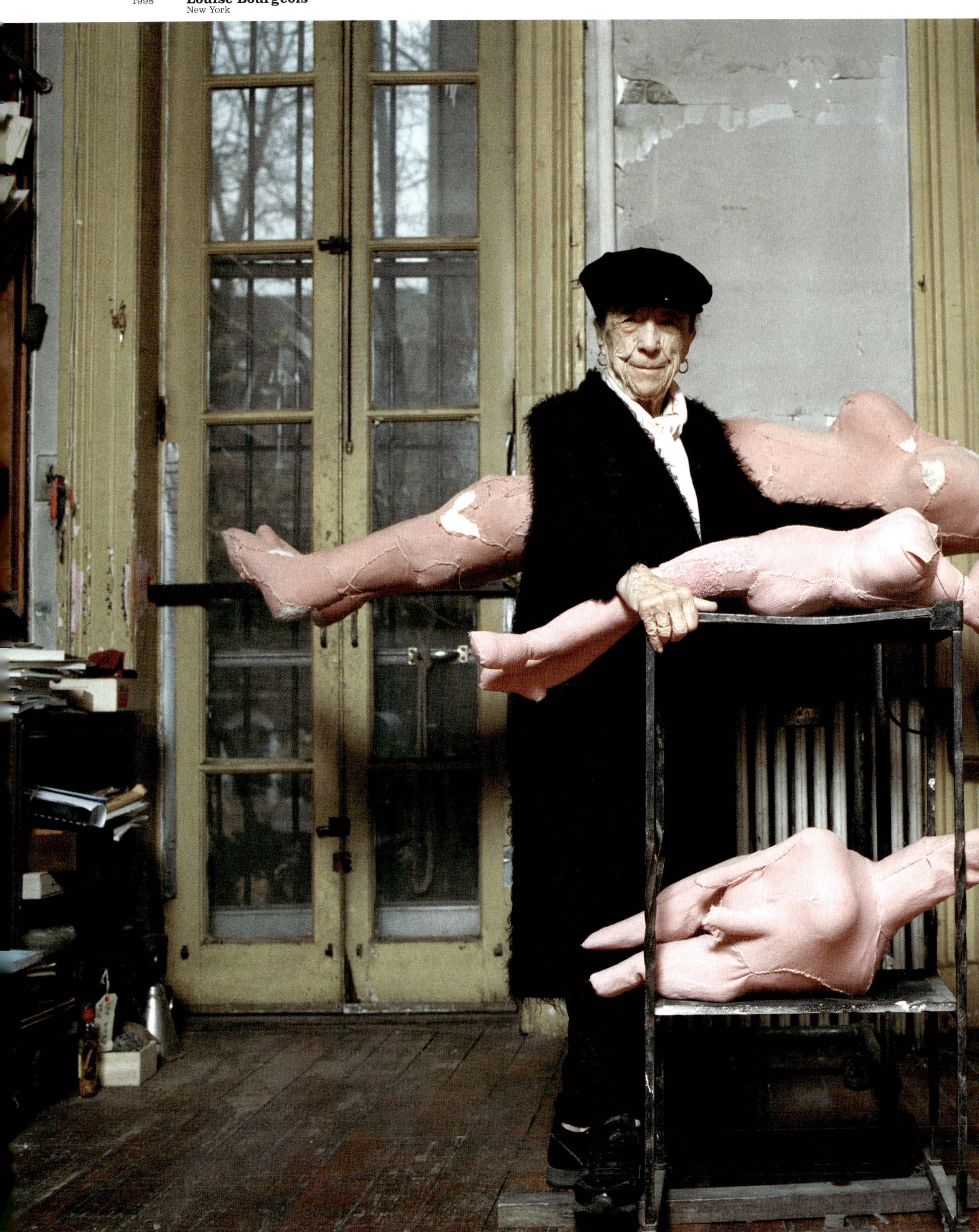

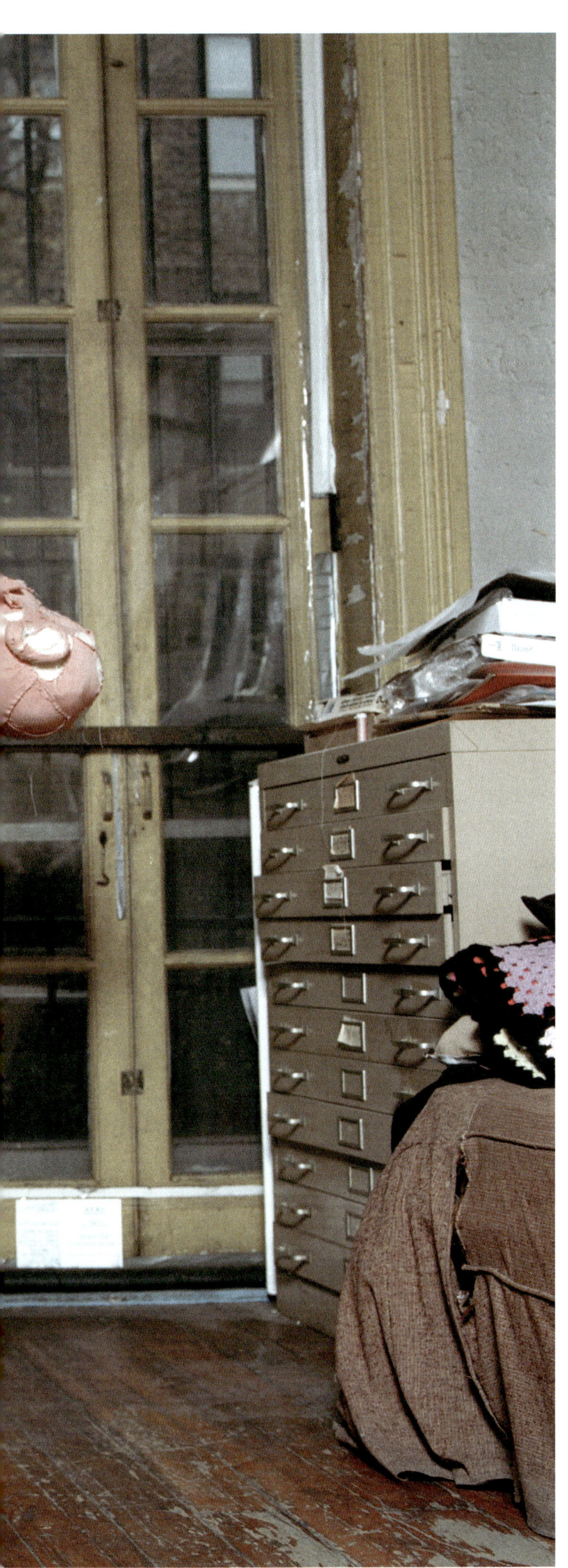

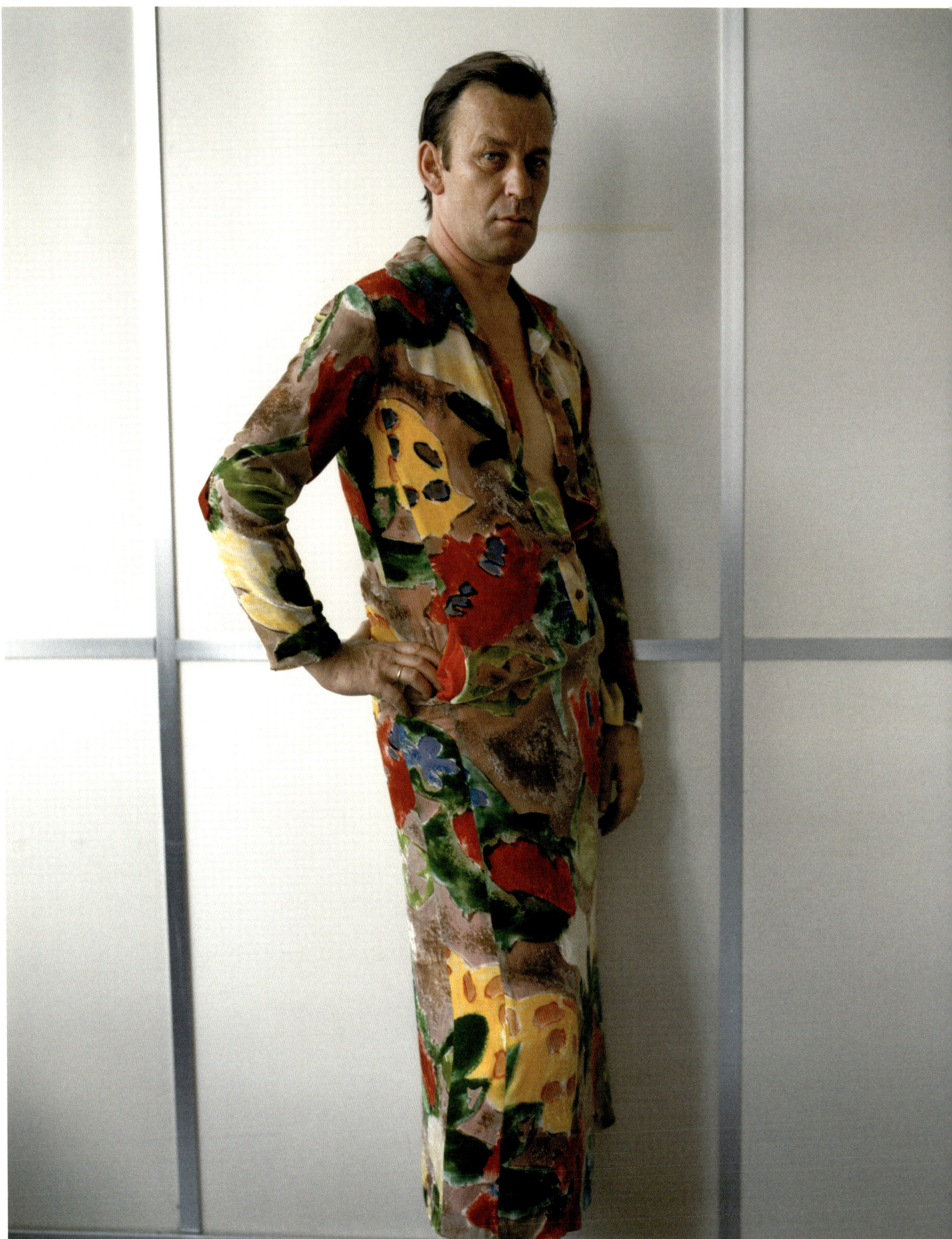

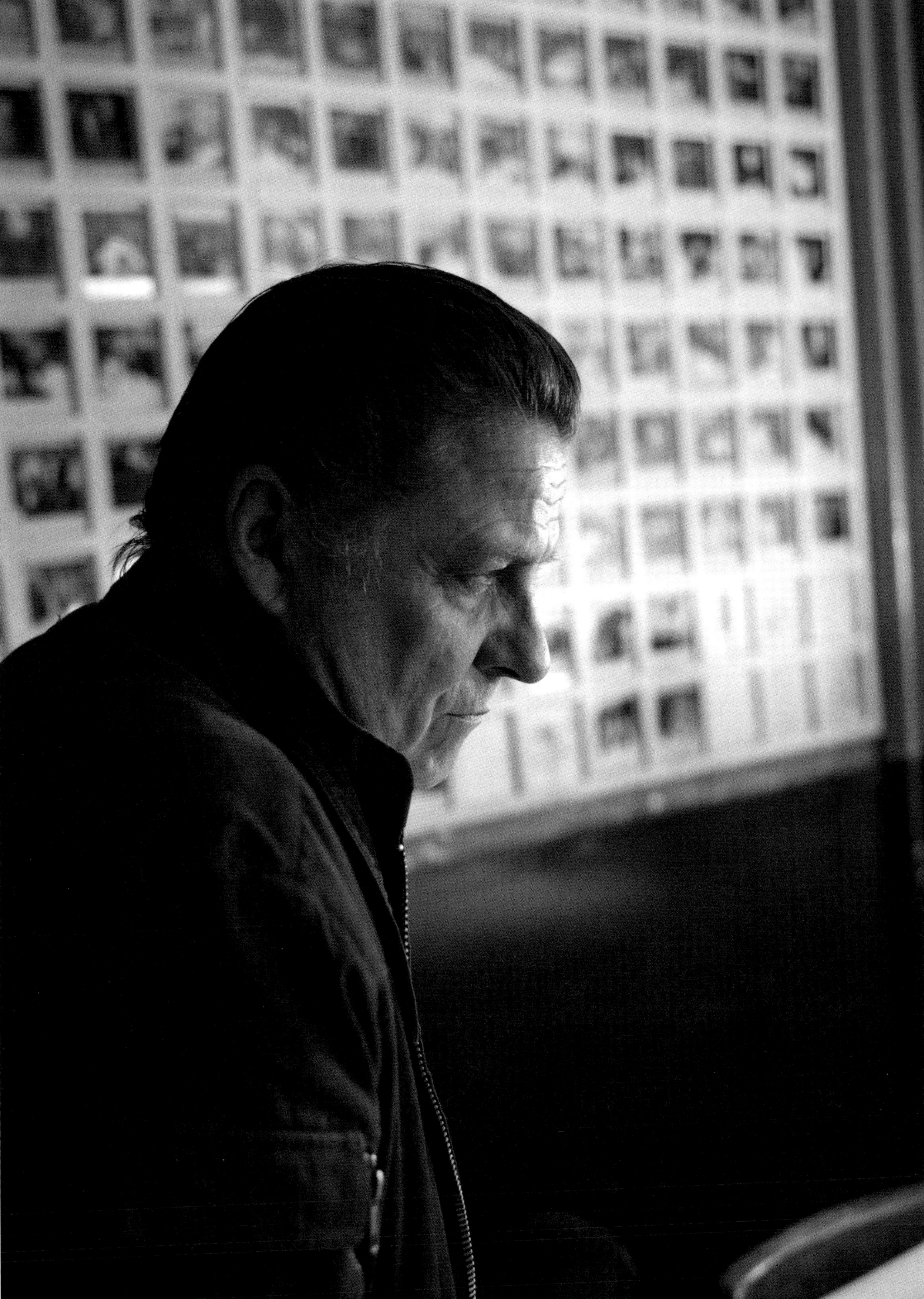

2009 **Georg Herold**
Berlin

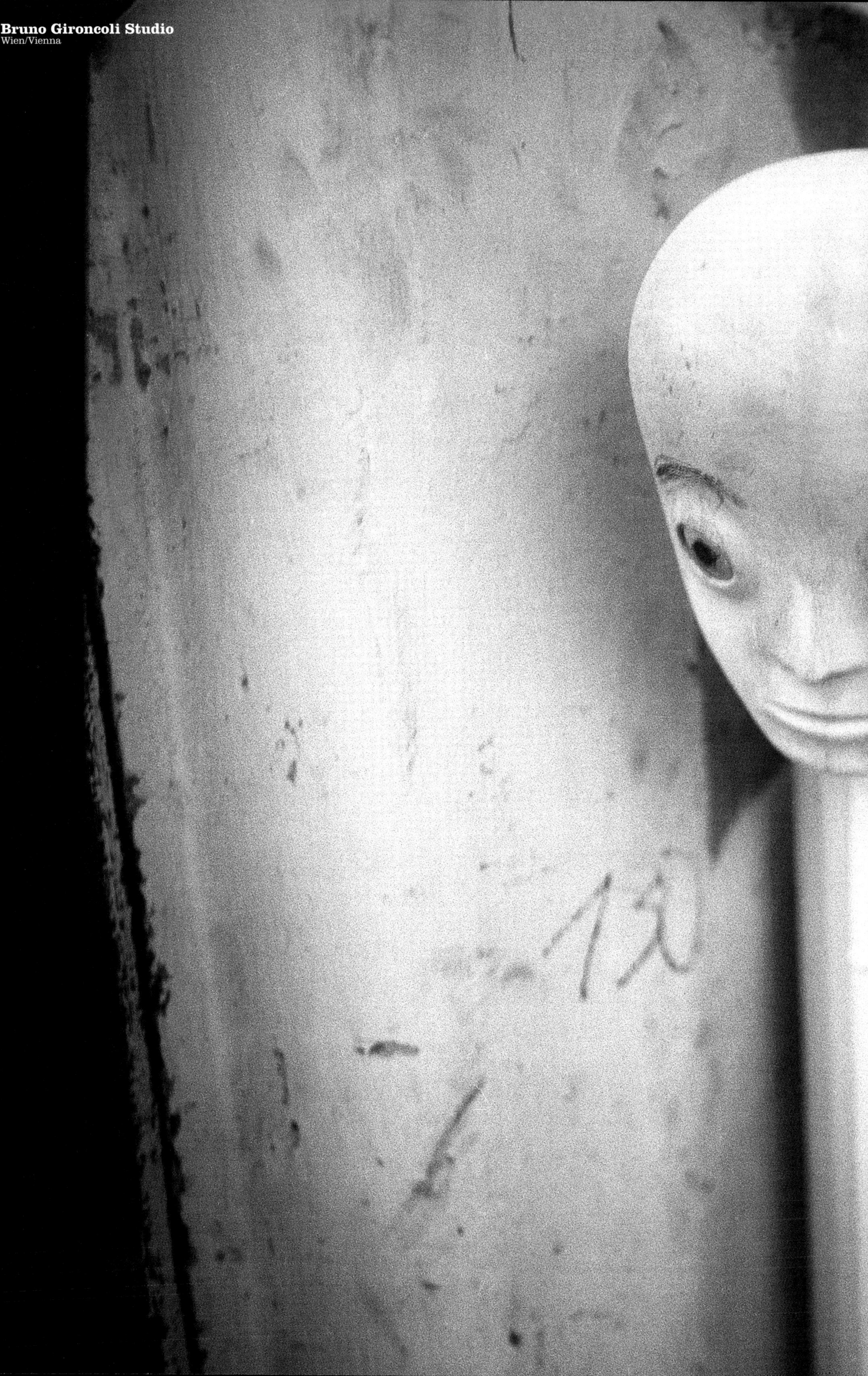

Bruno Gironcoli Studio
Wien/Vienna

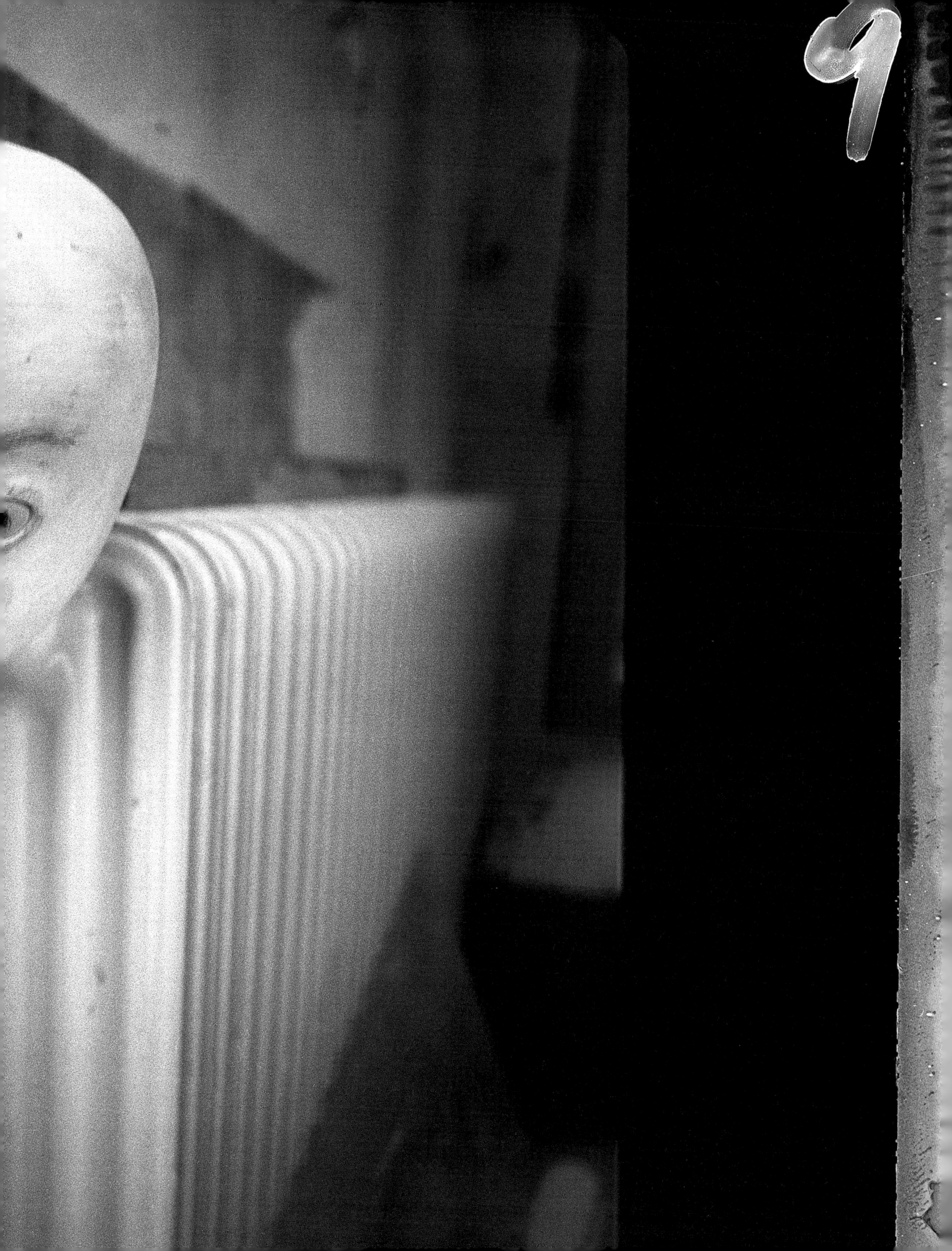
9

2009 **Norbert Schwontkowski**
Berlin

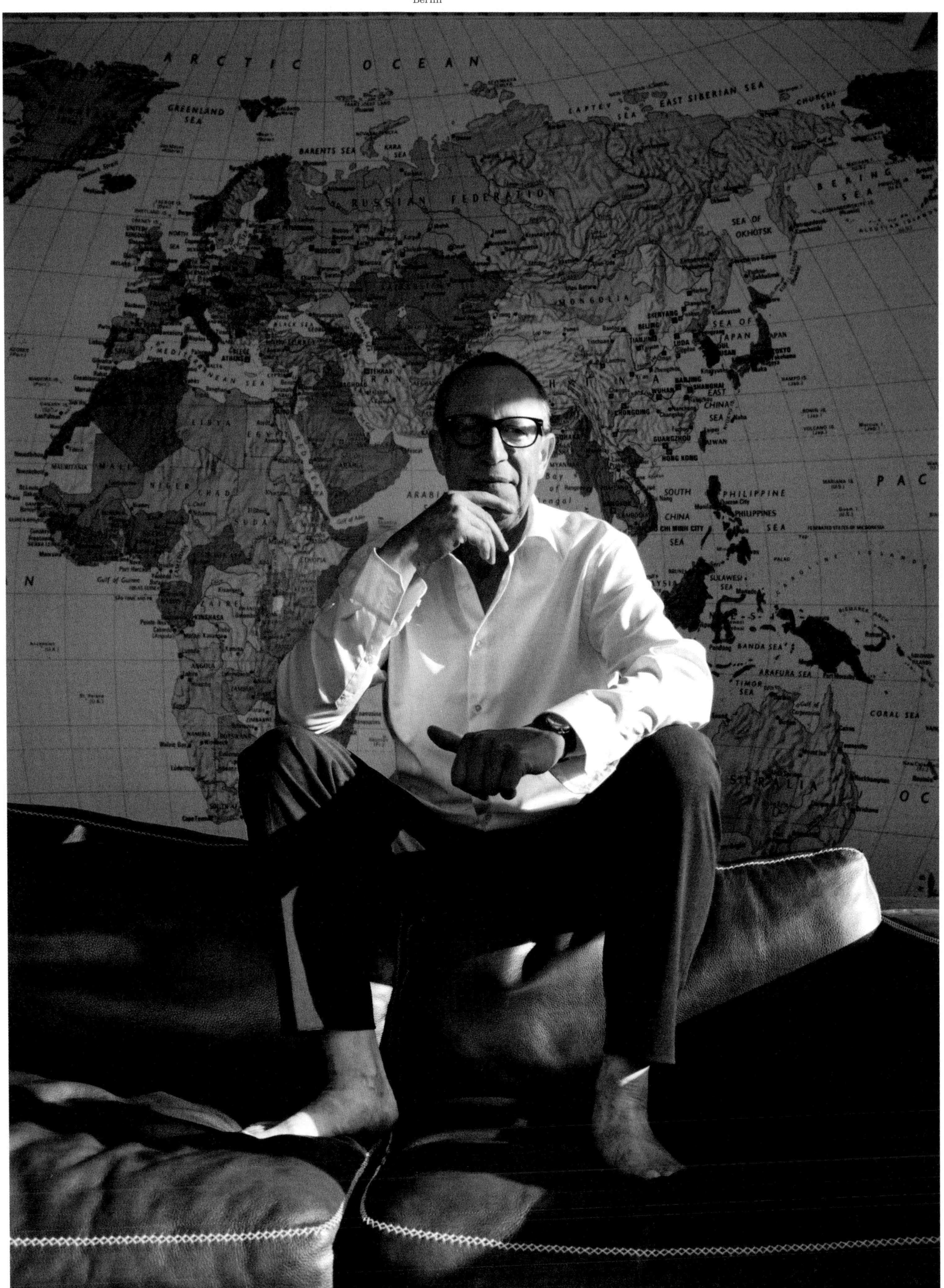

2006 **Elke Krystufek**
Wien/Vienna

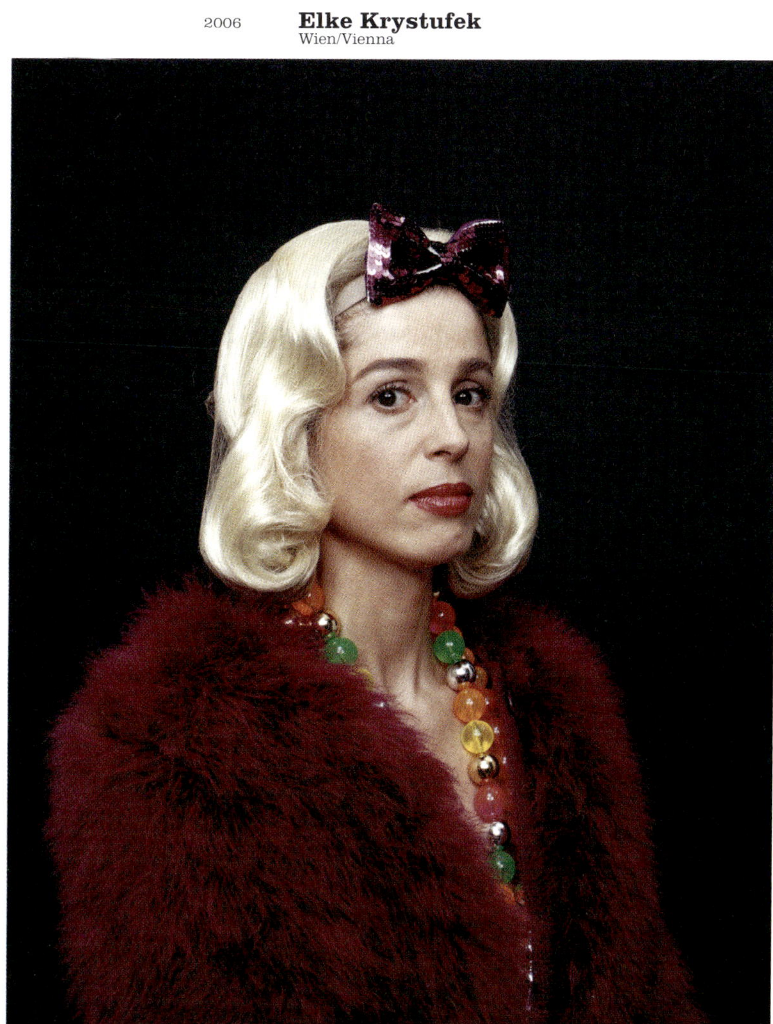

1995 **Bruno Gironcoli Studio**
Wien/Vienna

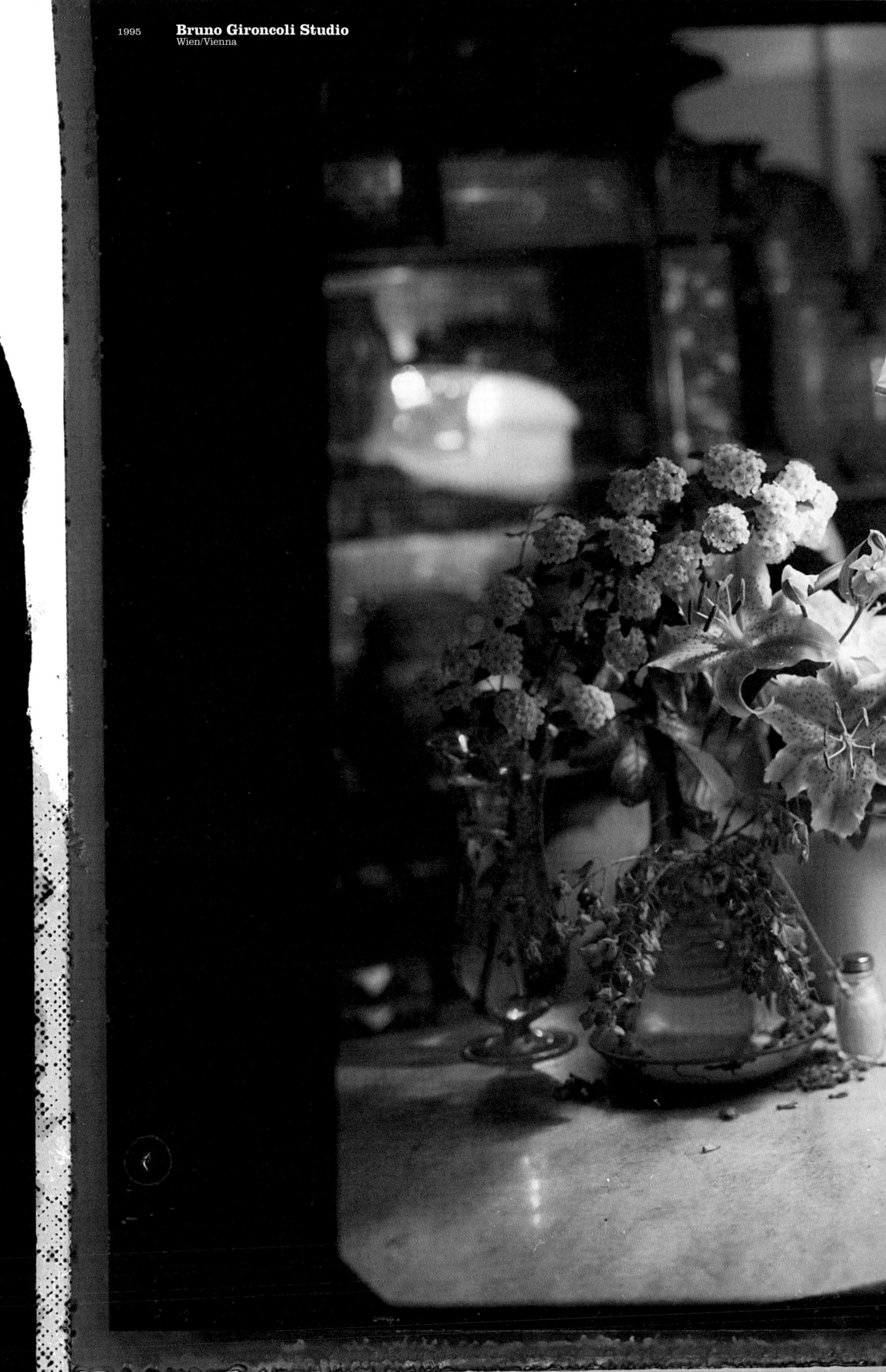

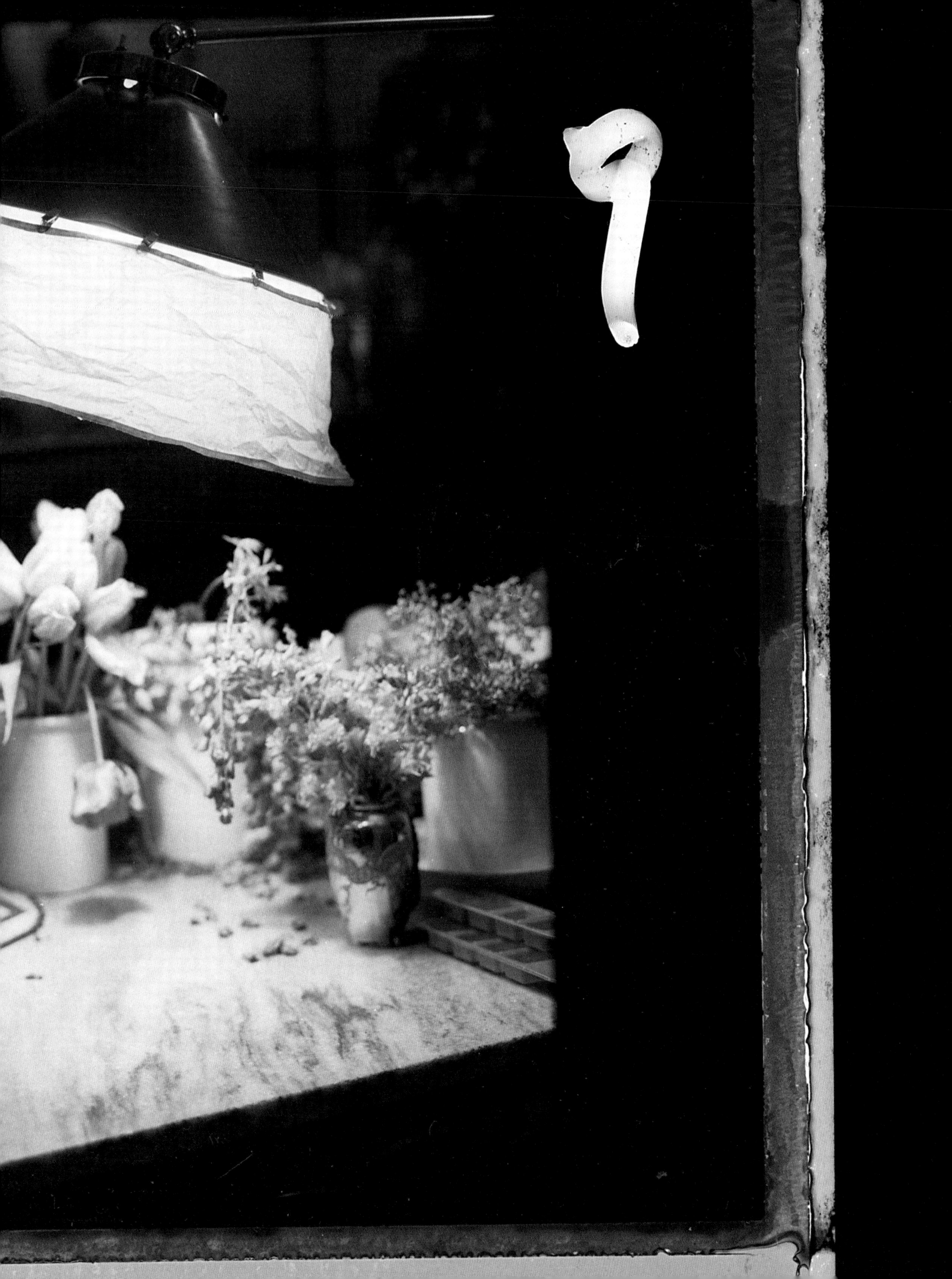

1988 **Erwin Wurm**
Wien/Vienna

2003 **Vladimir Dubossarsky/ Alexander Vinogradov**
Venedig/Venice

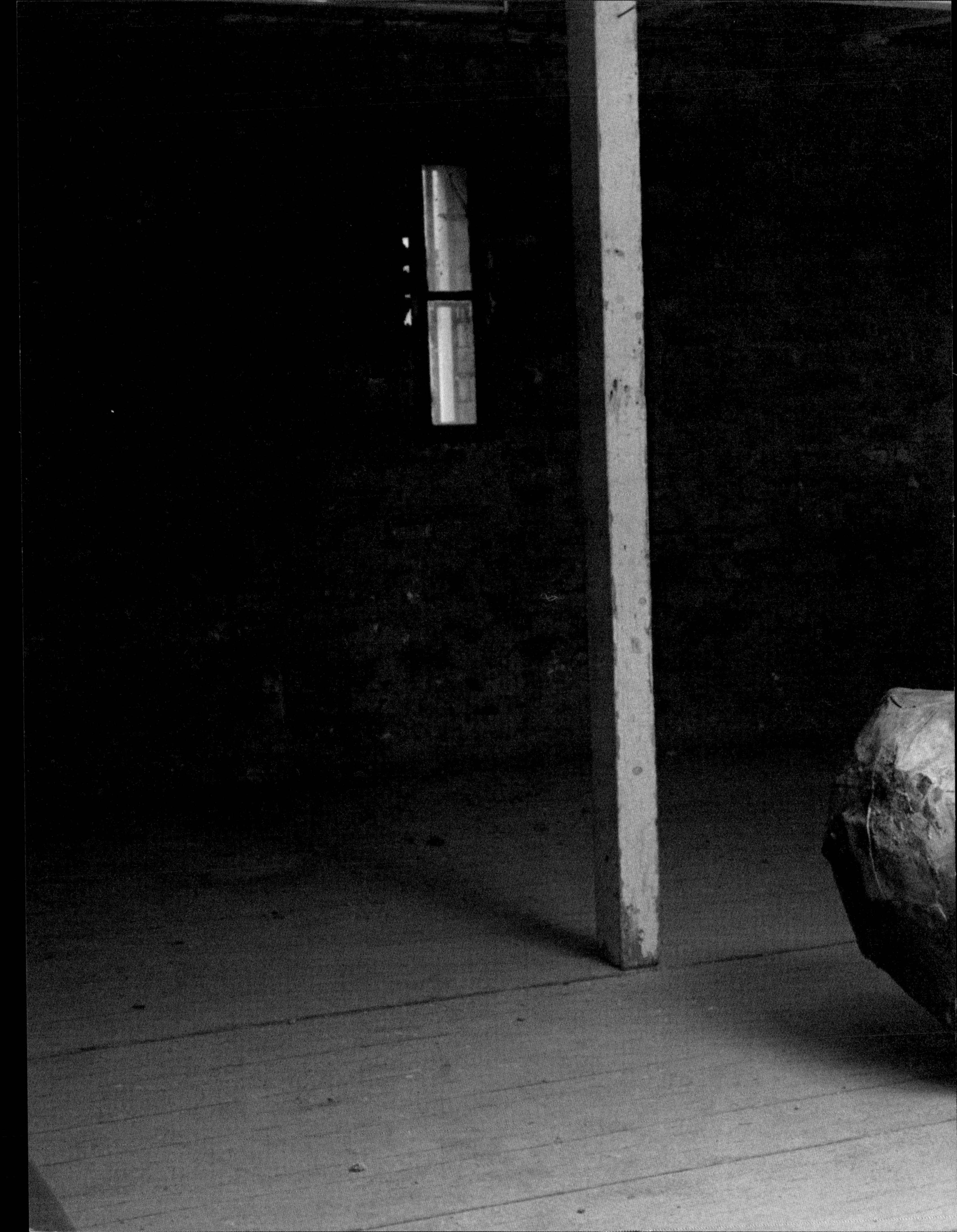

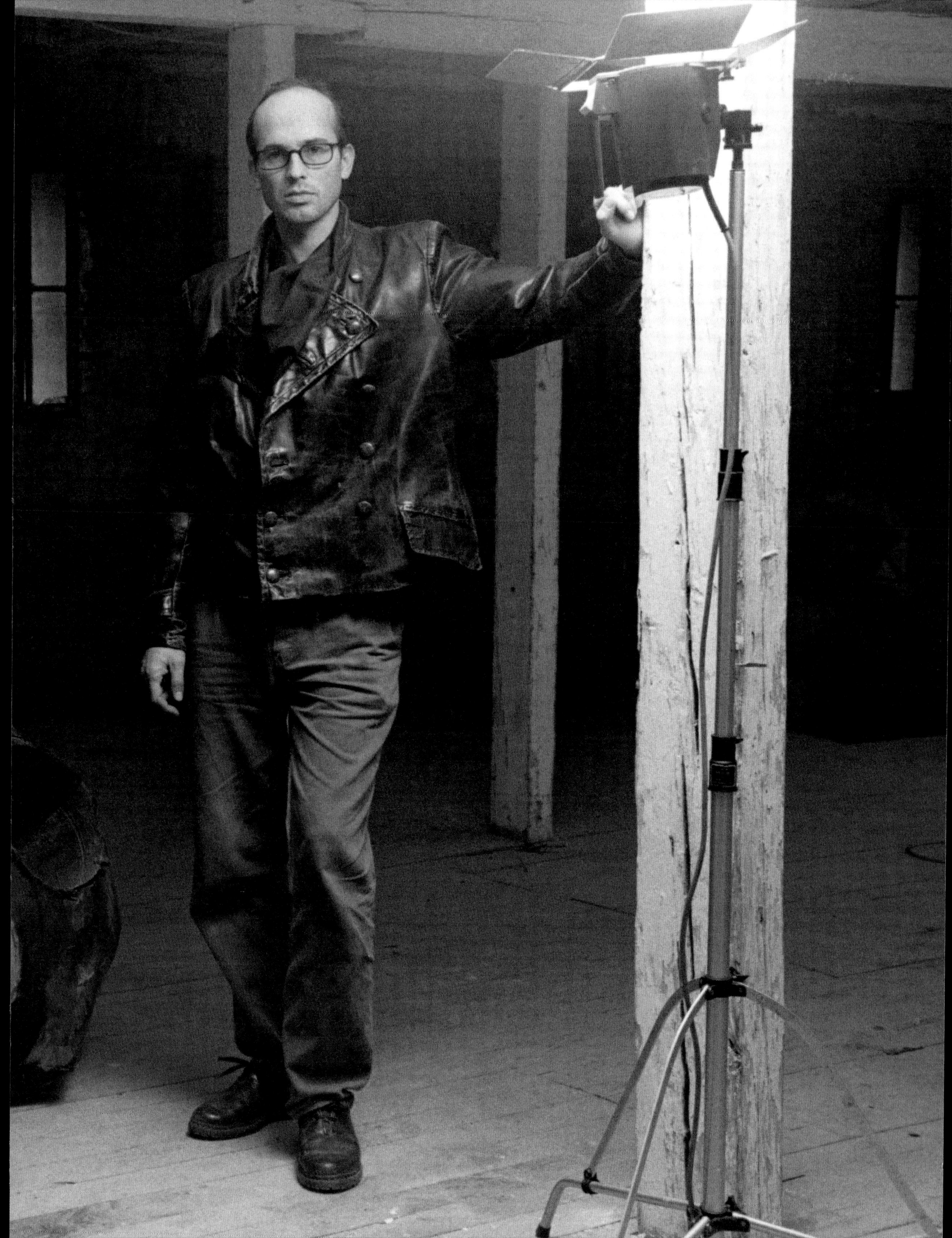

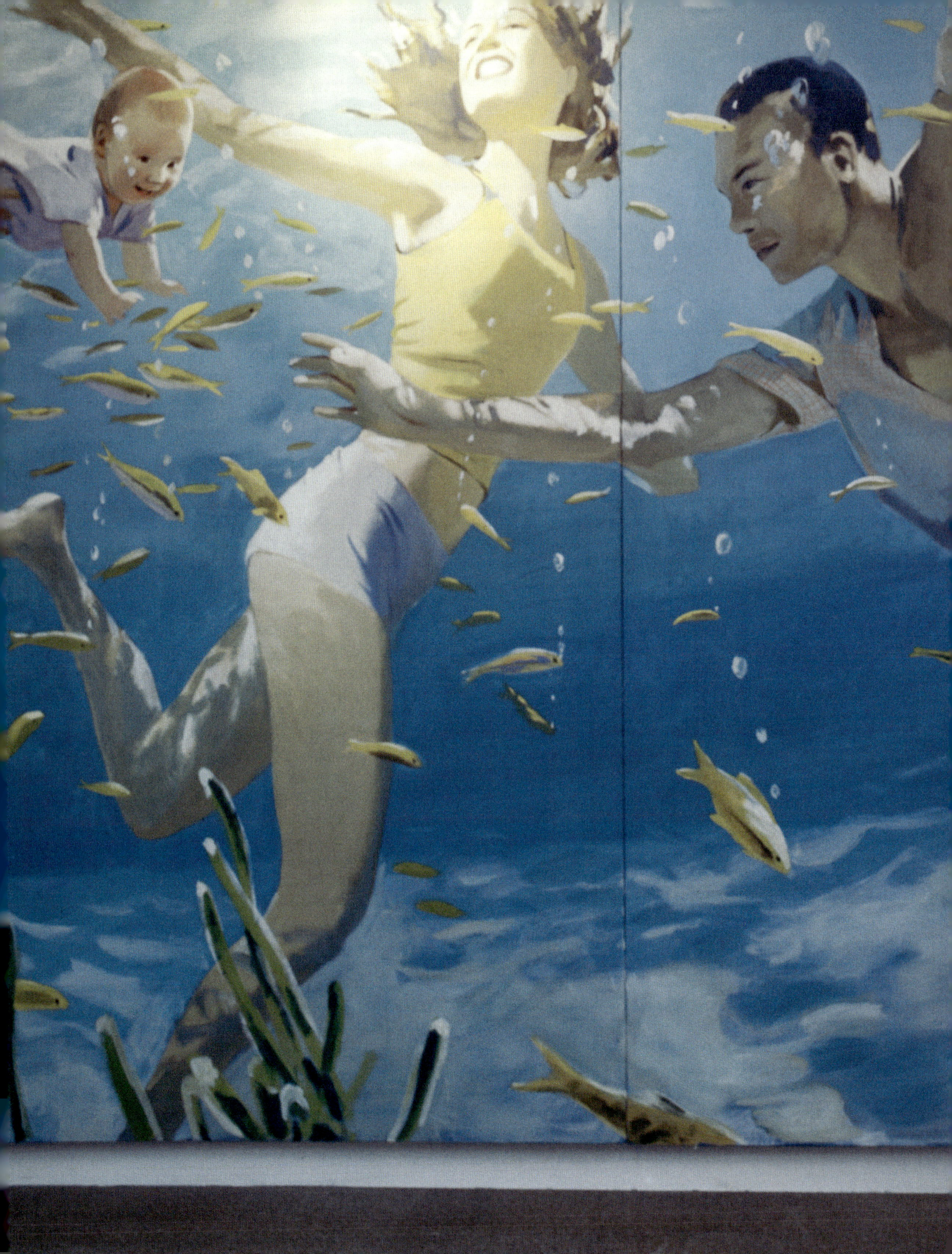

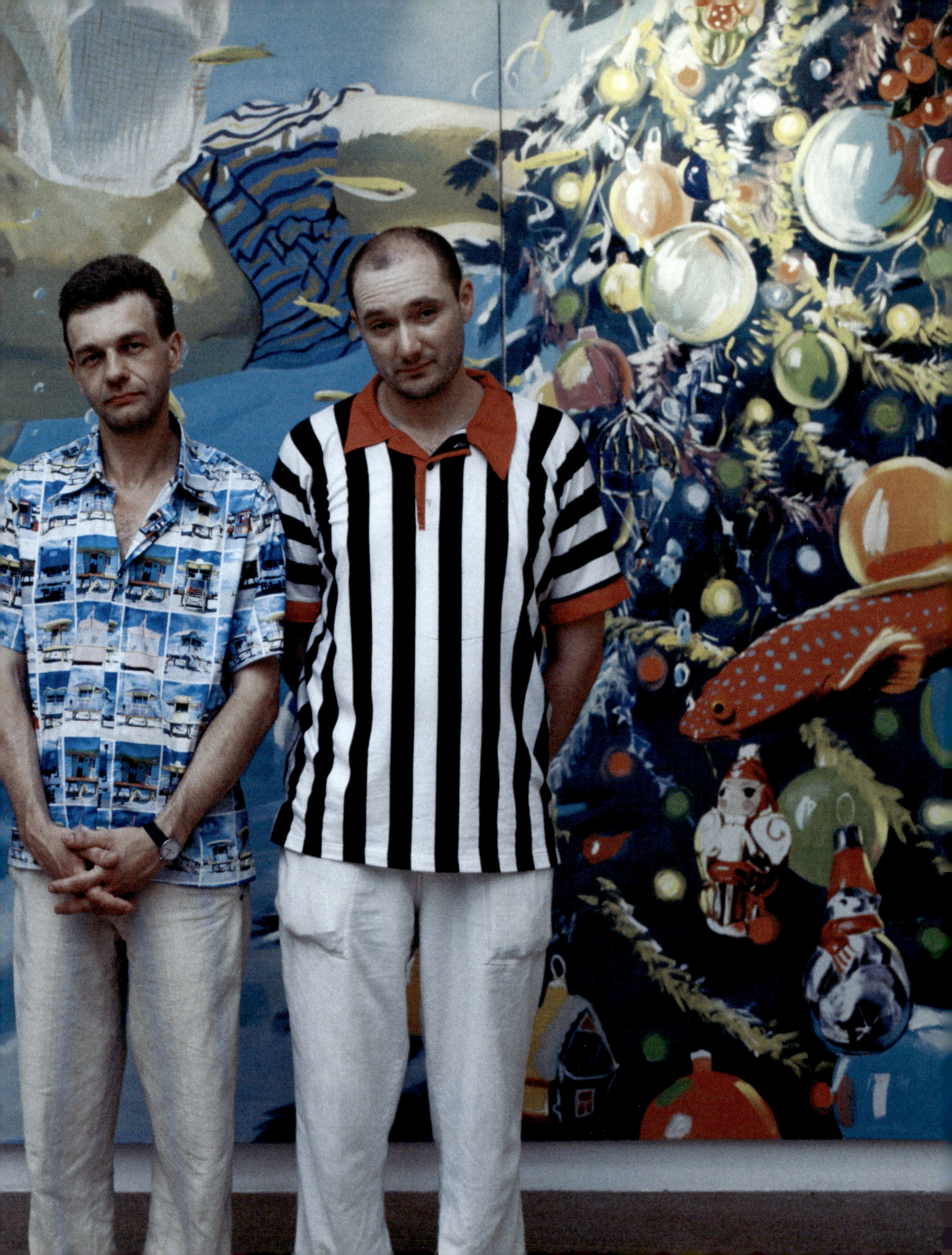

2003 **Marina Abramović**
Avignon

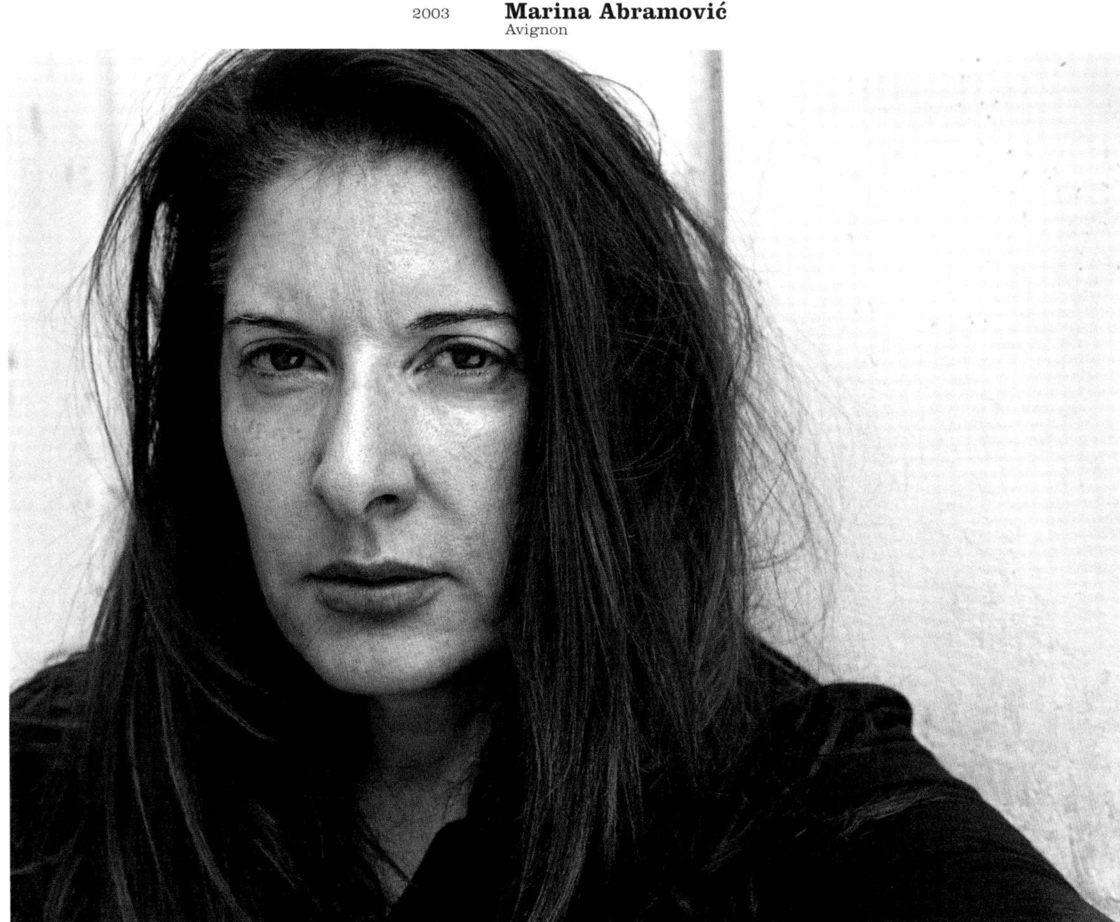

2003 **Christopher Wool**
New York

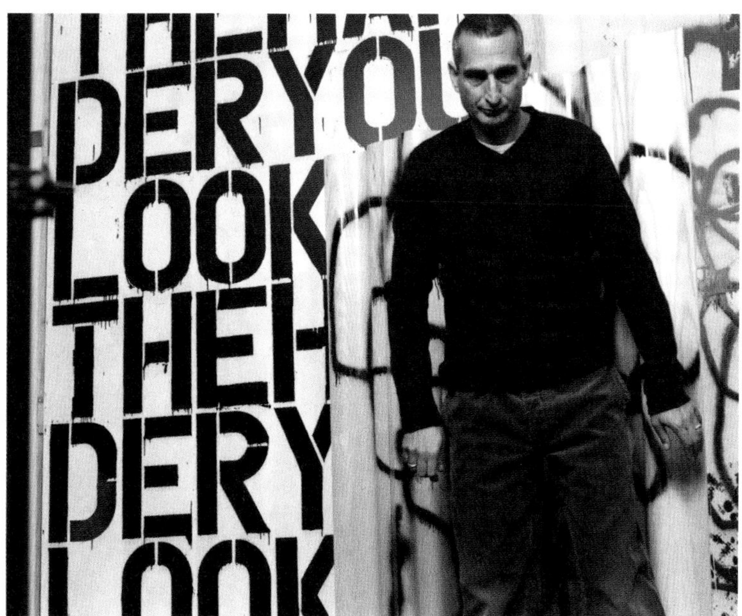

1988 **Michael Kienzer Studio**
Wien/Vienna

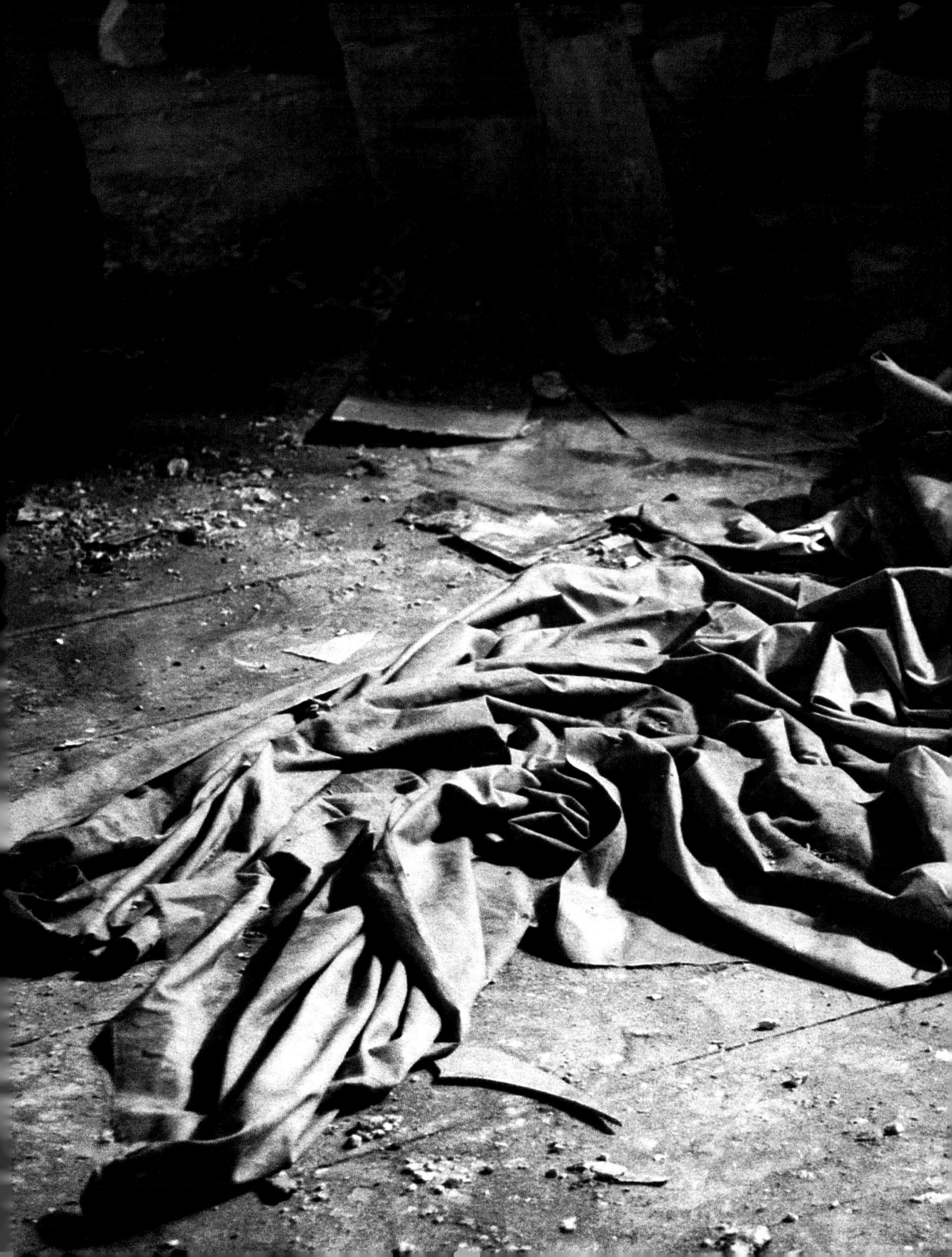

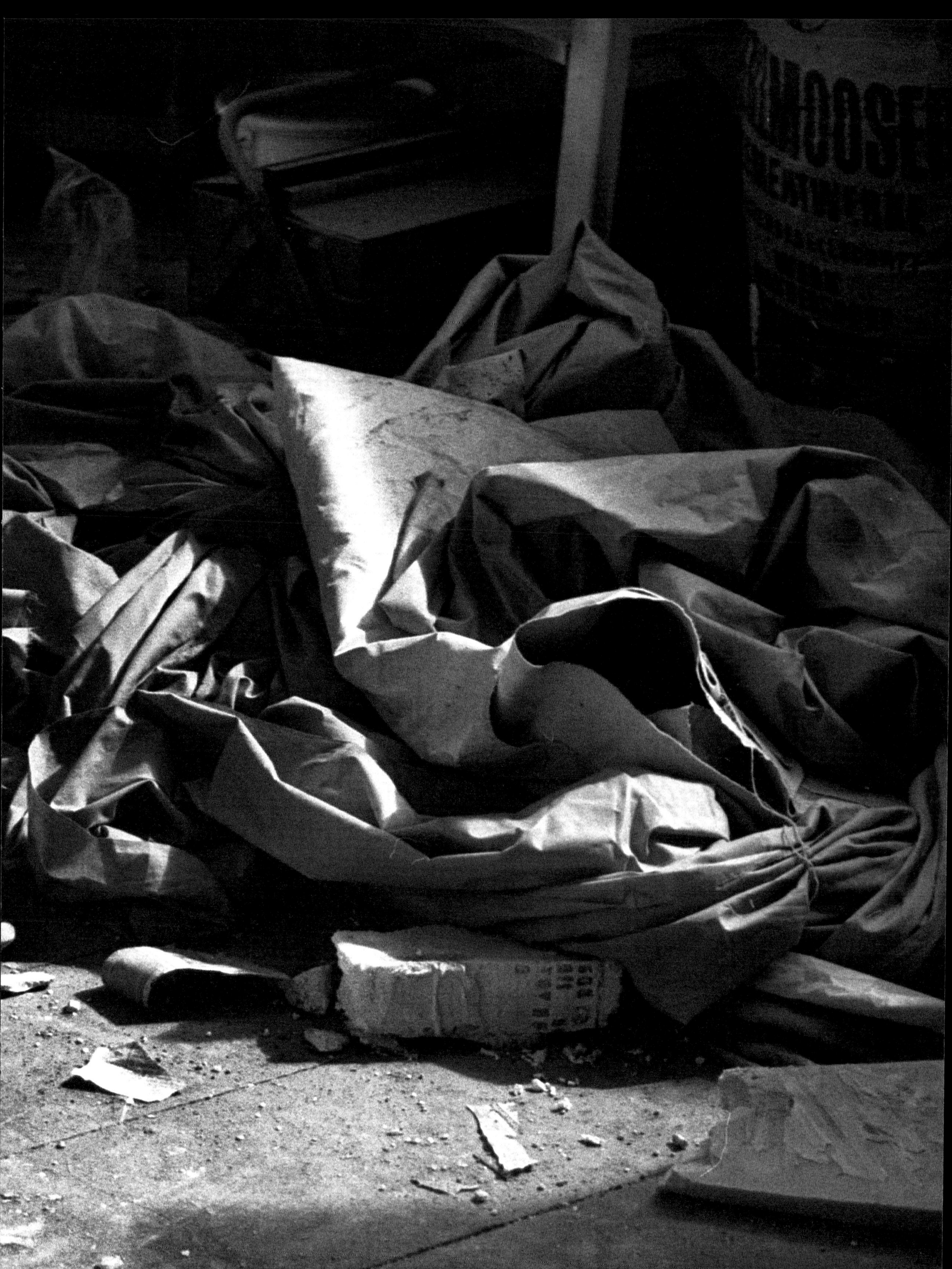

2008 **Marc Brandenburg**
Berlin

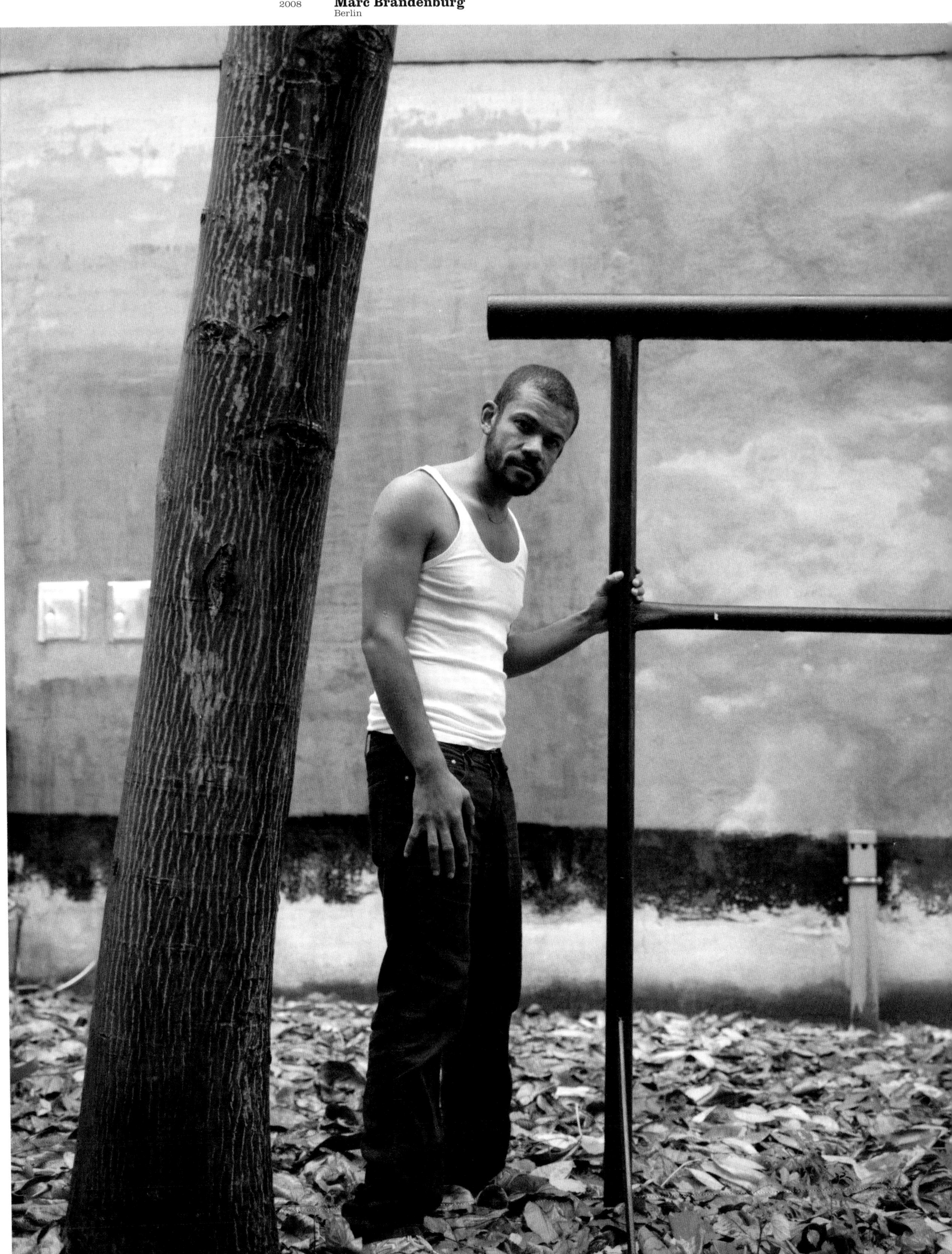

Walter Pichler
Wien/Vienna

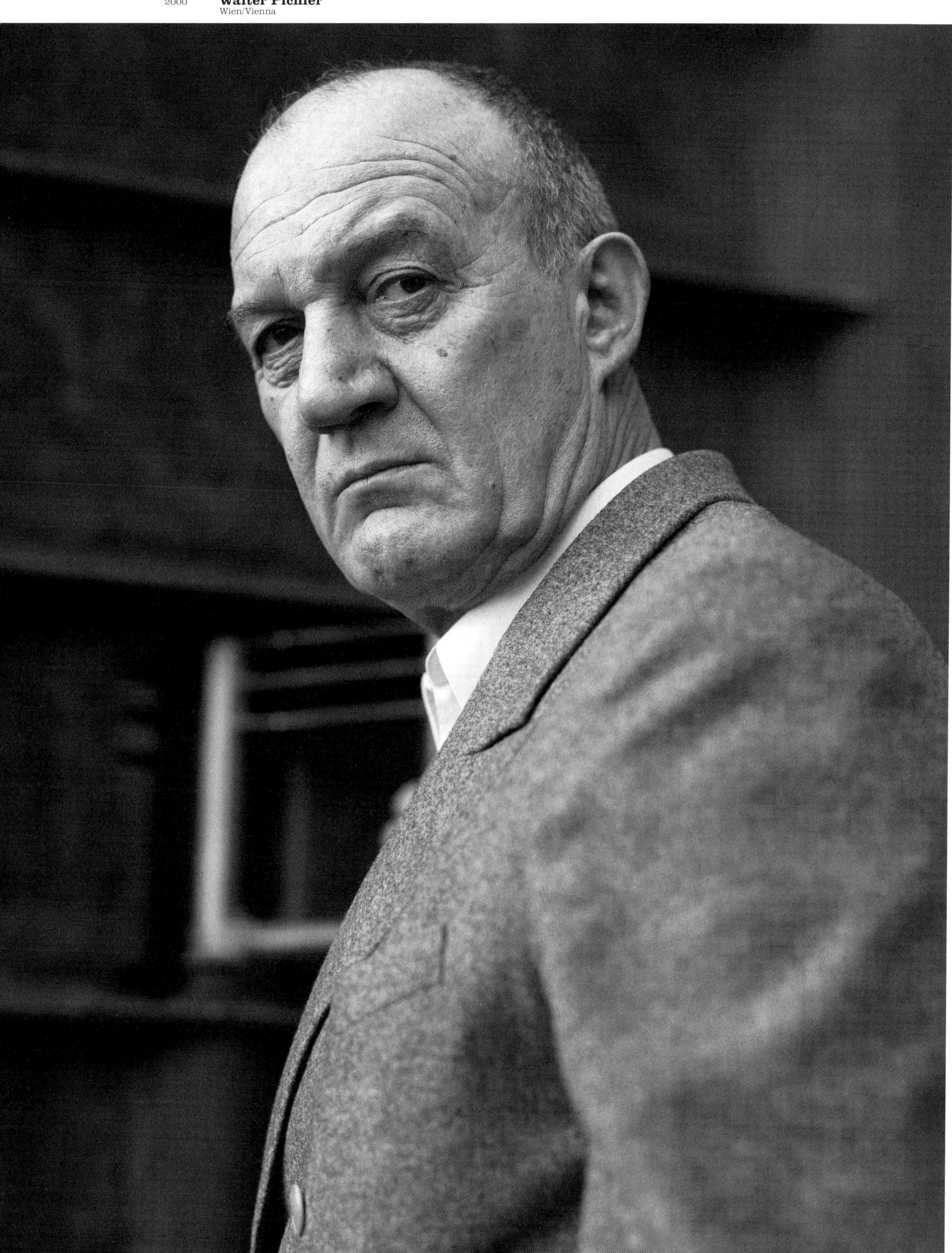

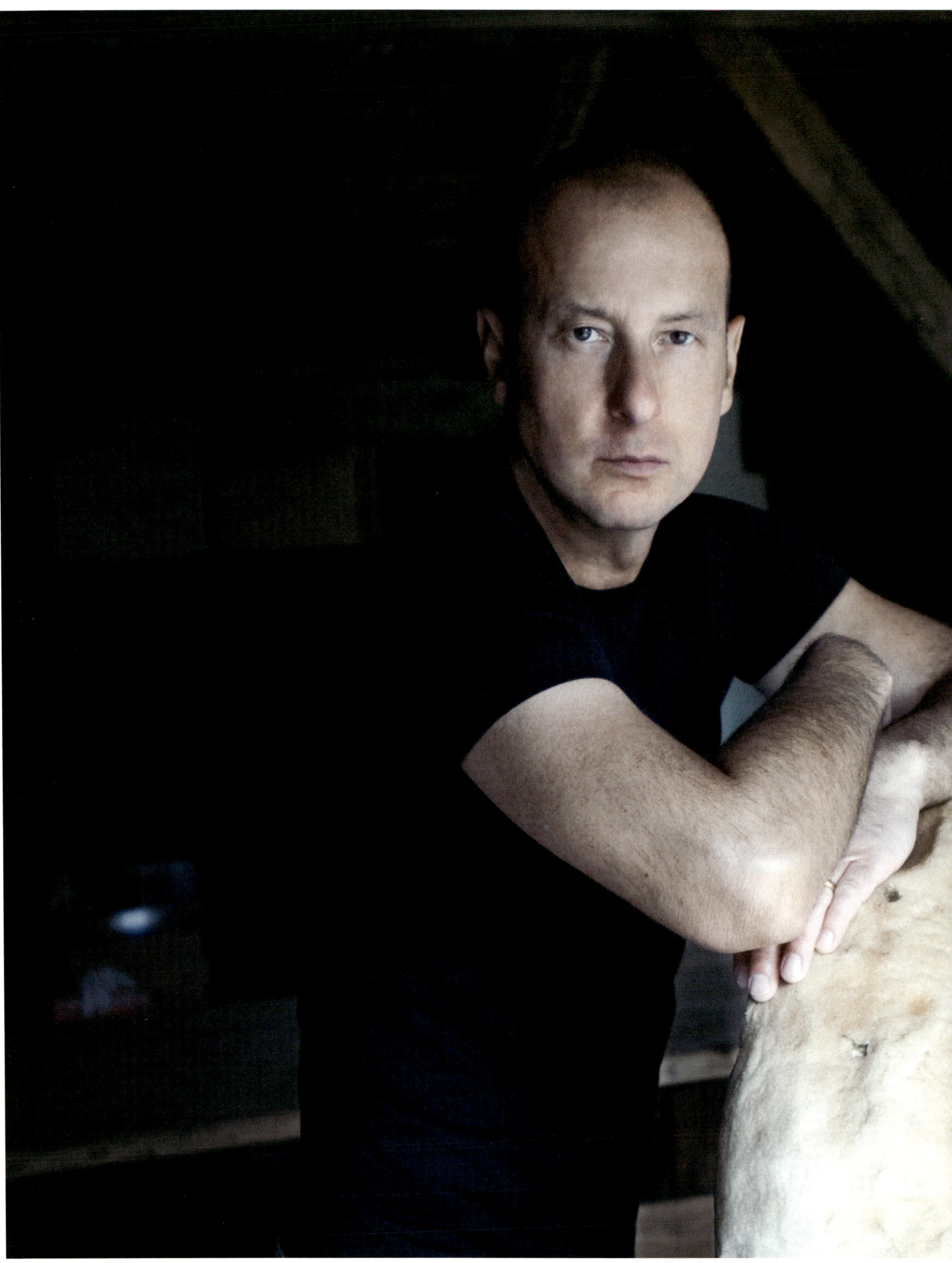

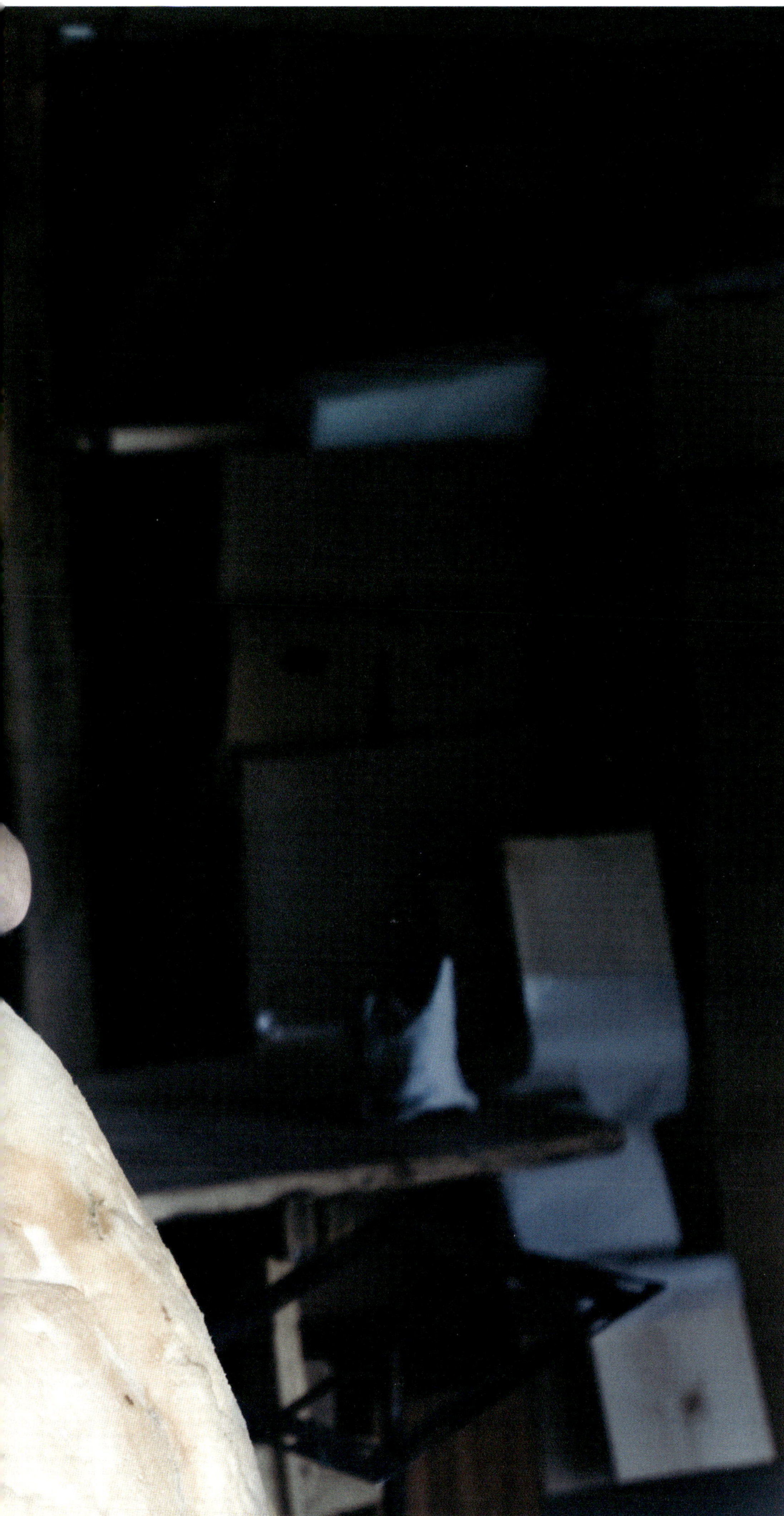

2010 **Helmut Lang**
Long Island

Vanessa Beecroft
New York

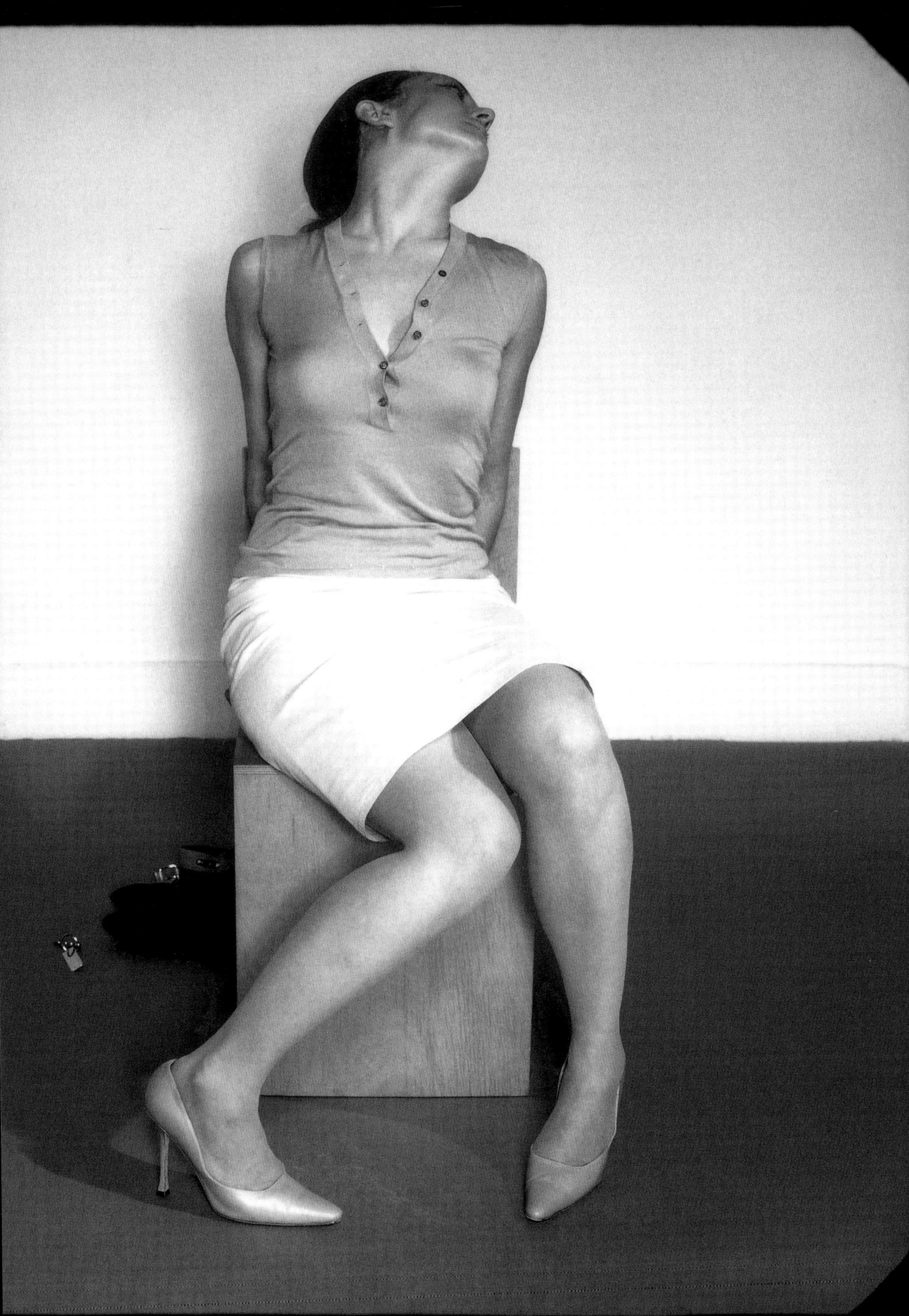

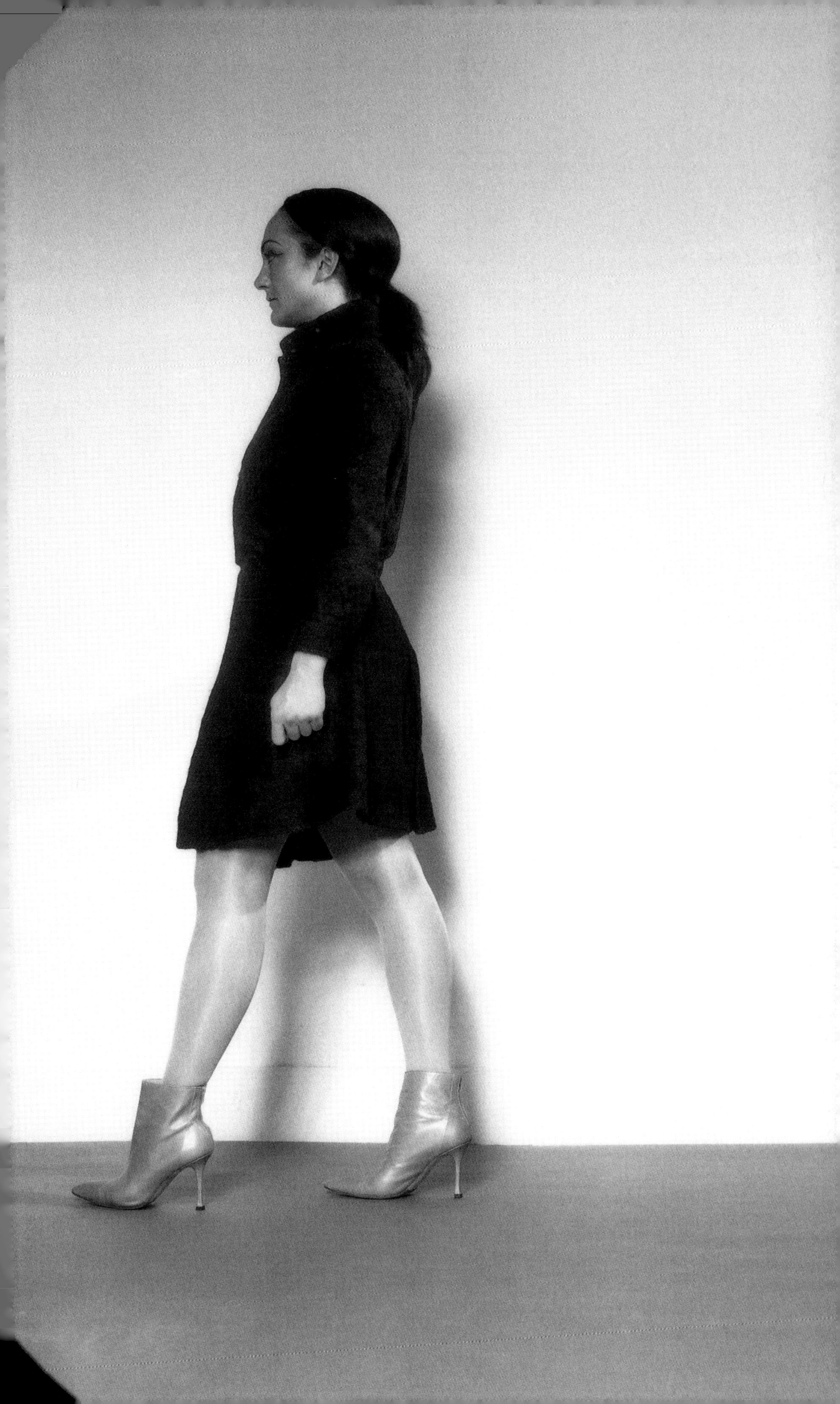

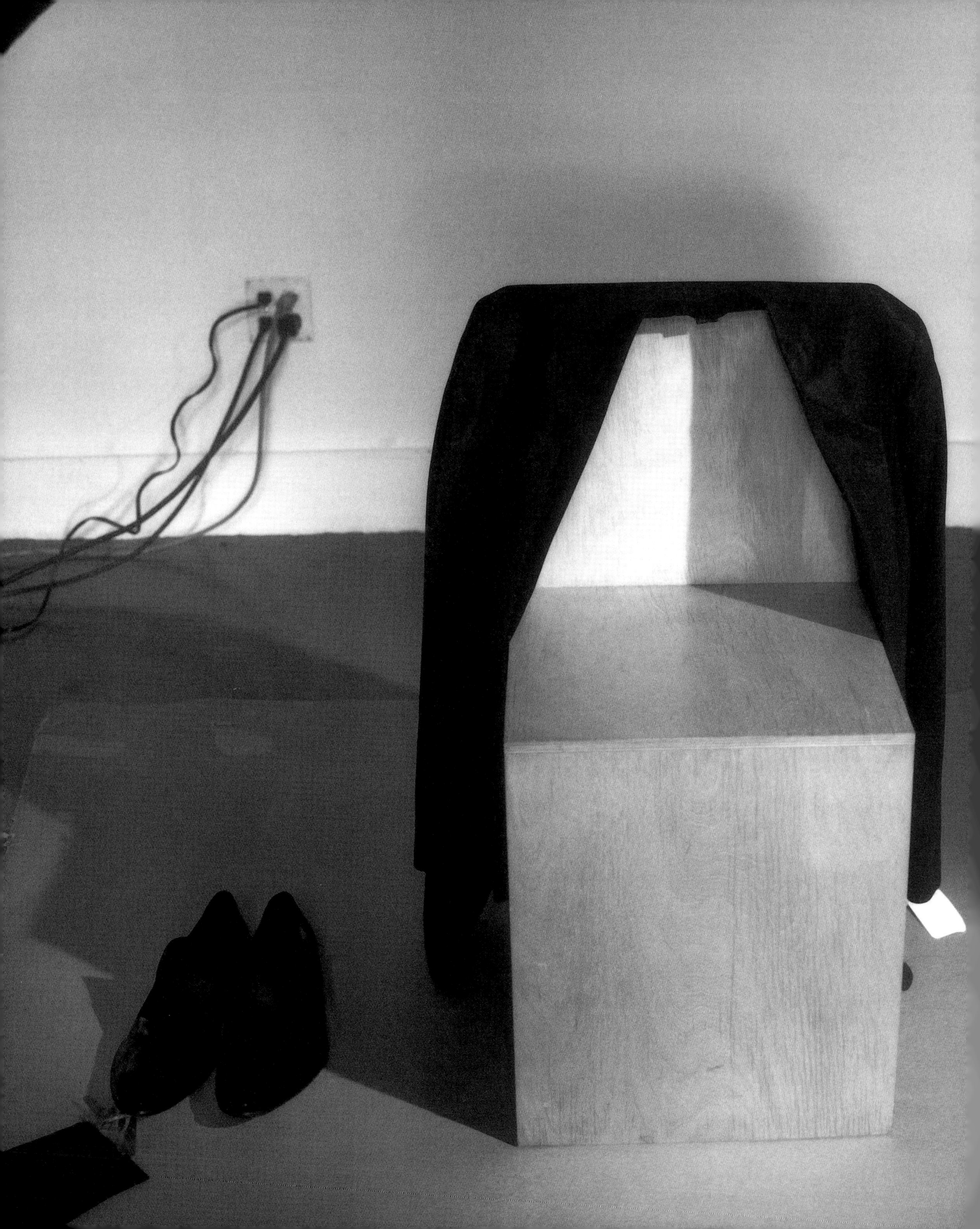

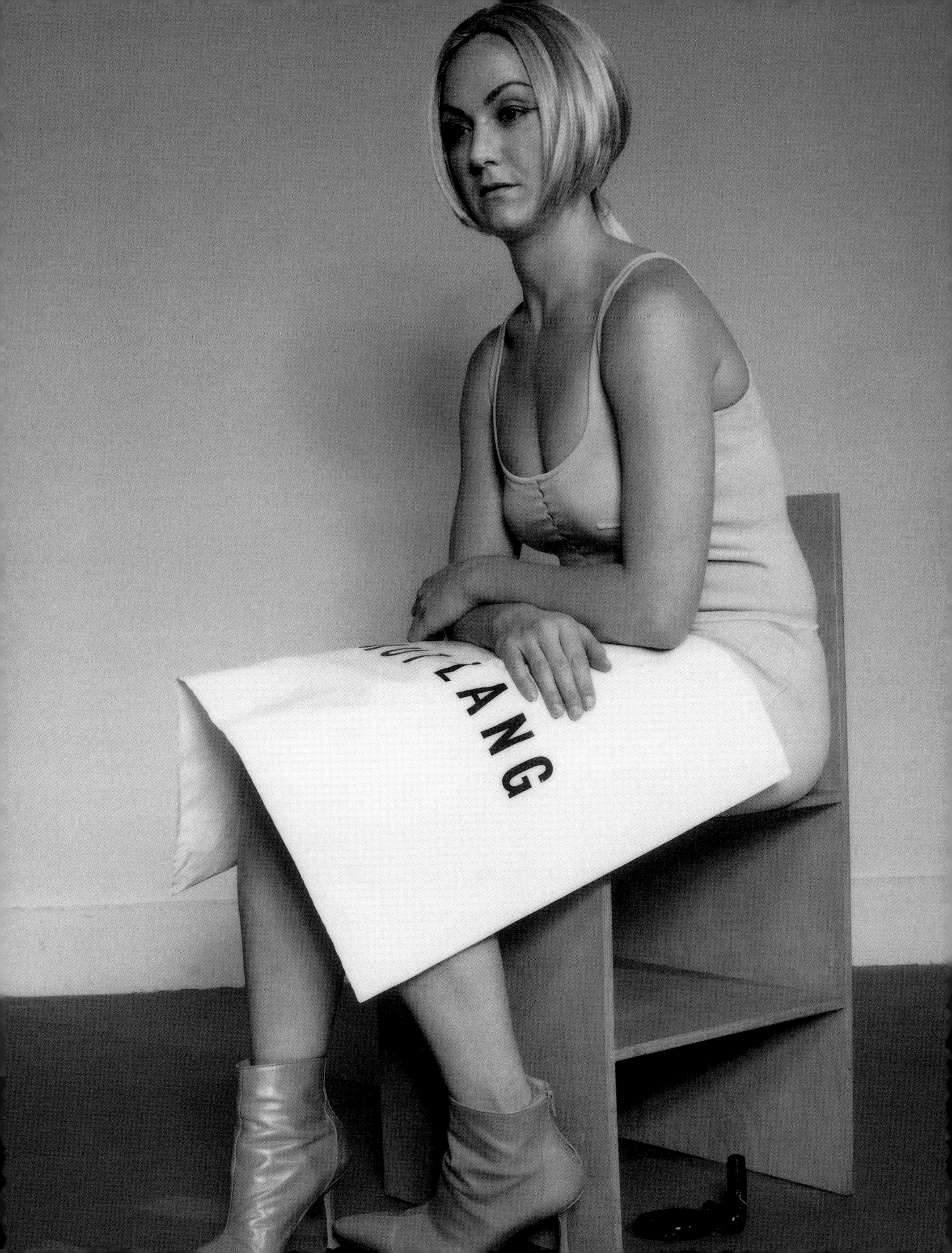
LANG

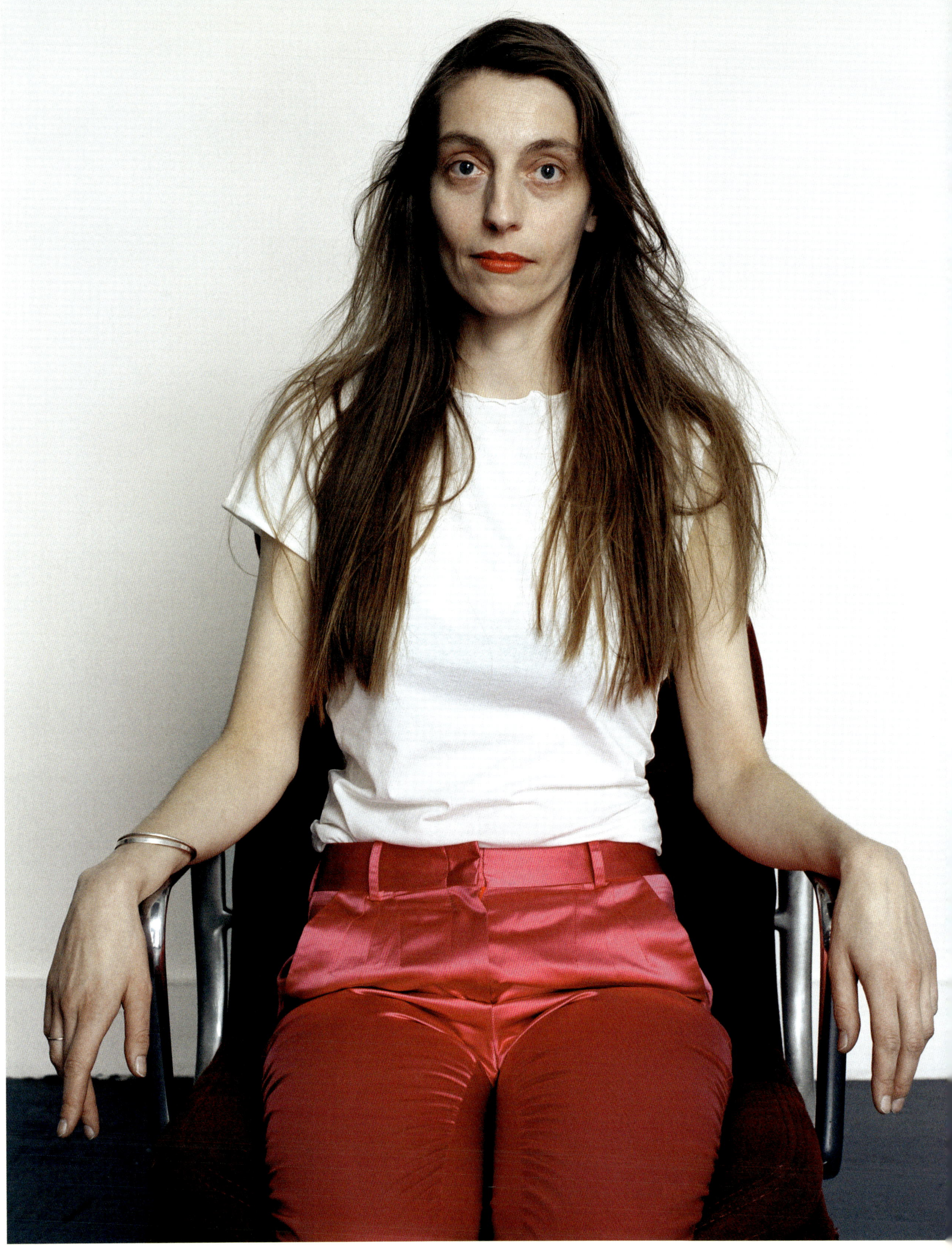

2008 **Tal R**
Kopenhagen/Copenhagen

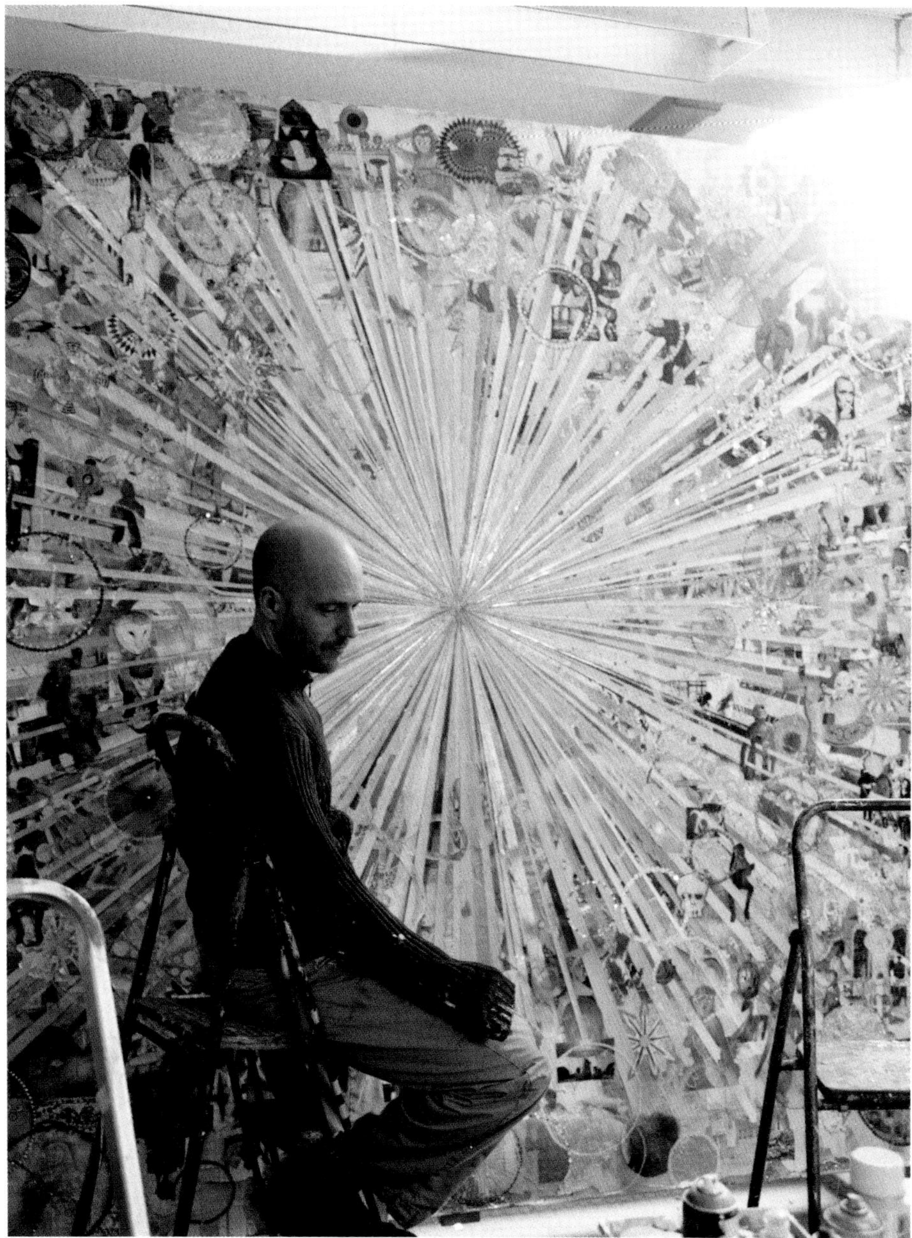

1990 **Kurt Kocherscheidt**
Bratislava

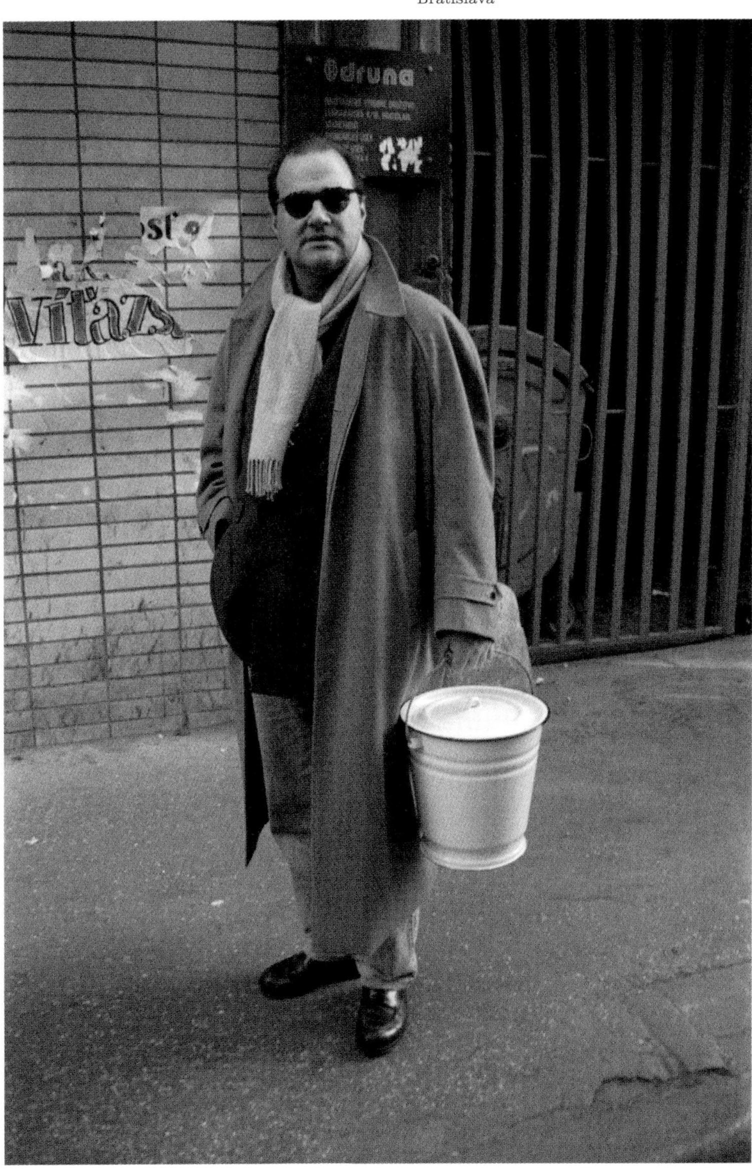

2000 **Hubert Scheibl**
Wien/Vienna

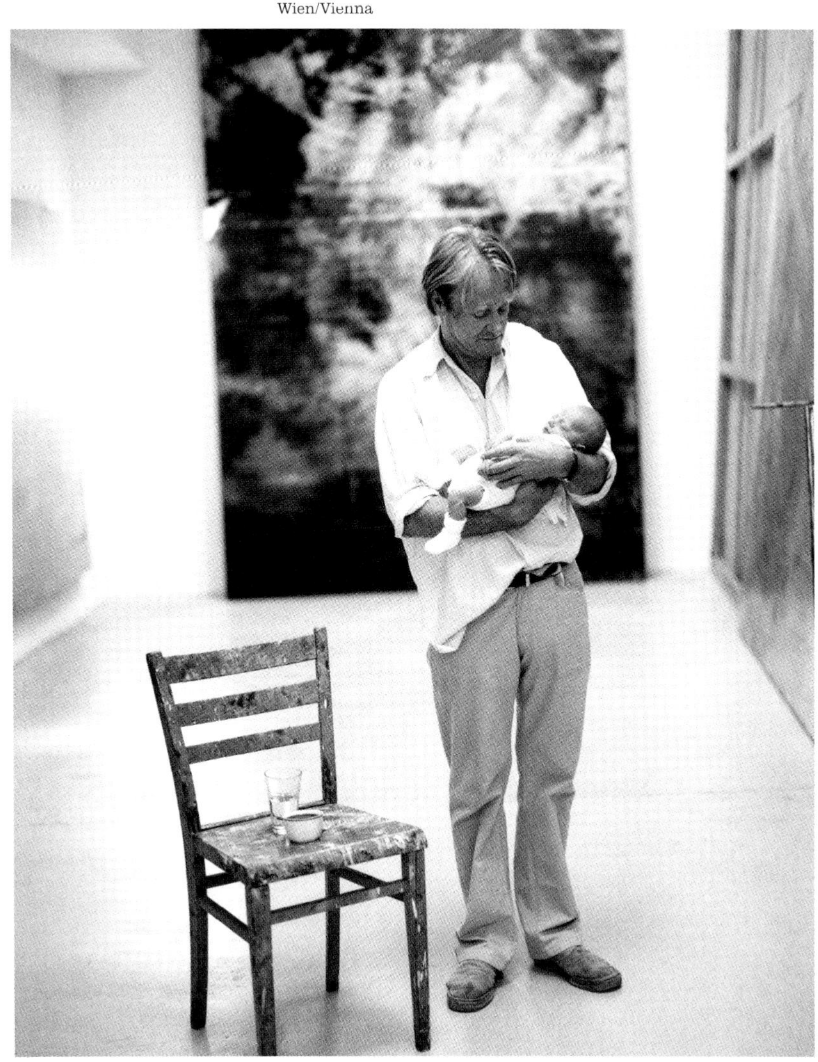

1995 **Bruno Gironcoli**
Wien/Vienna

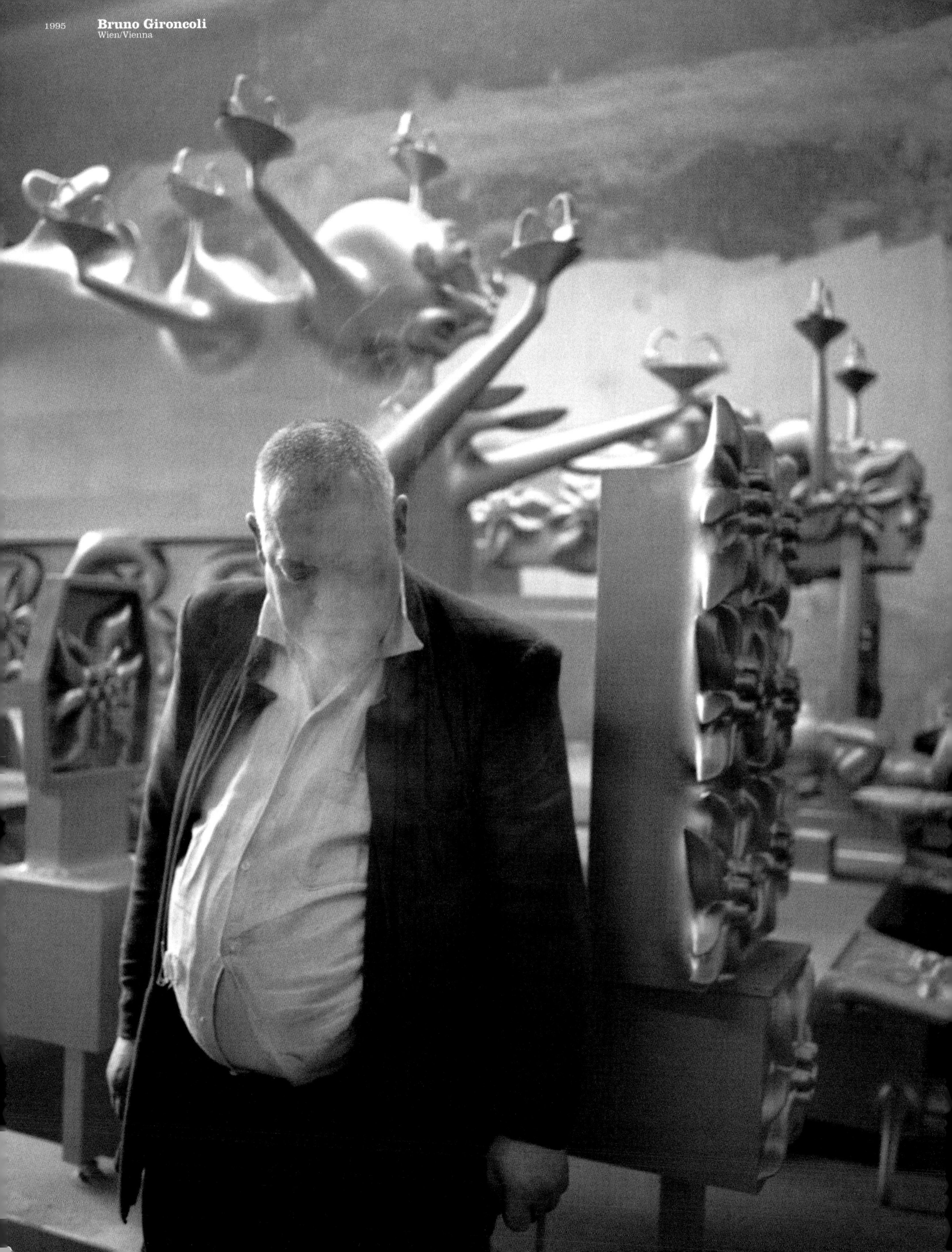

Bruno Gironcoli Studio
Wien/Vienna

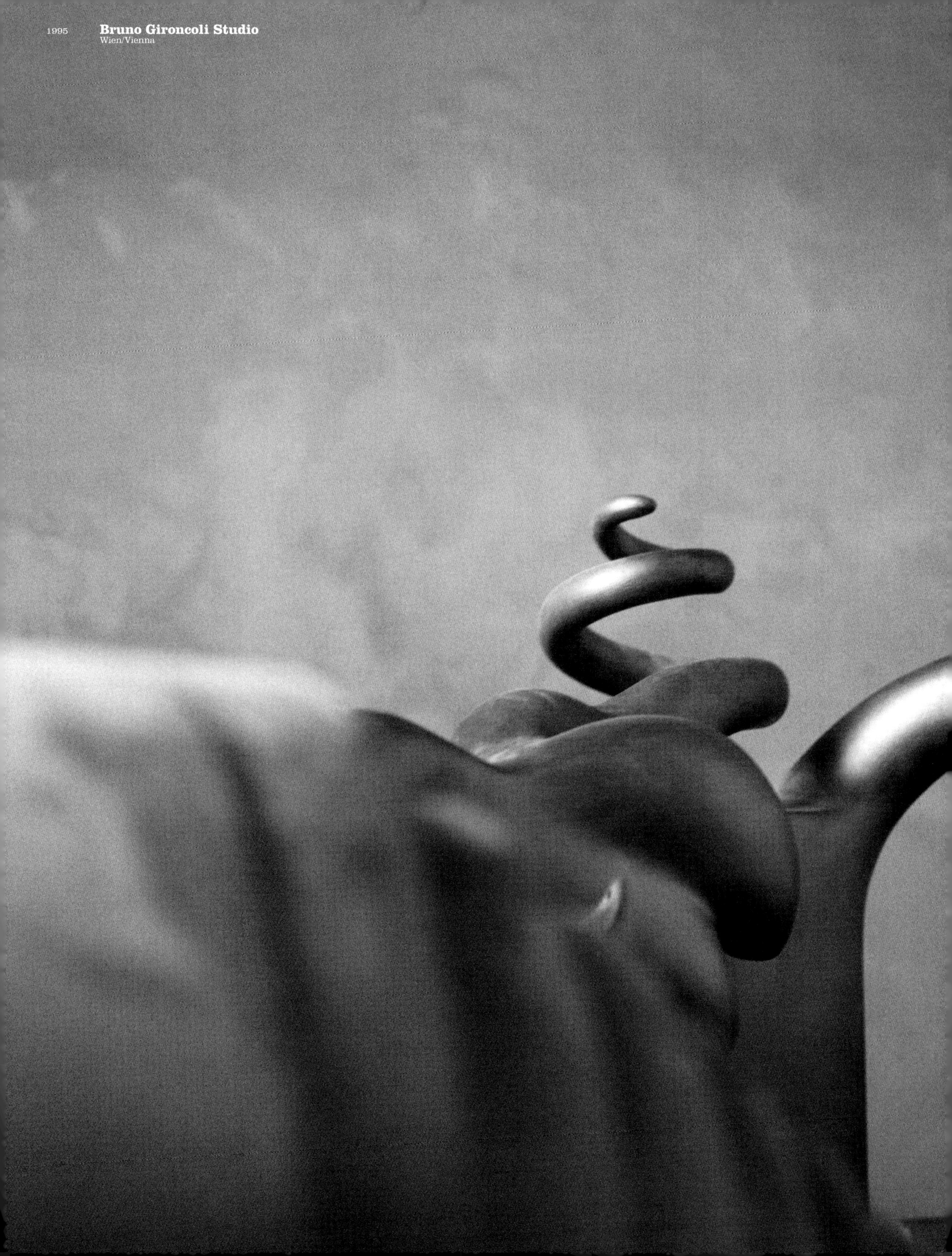

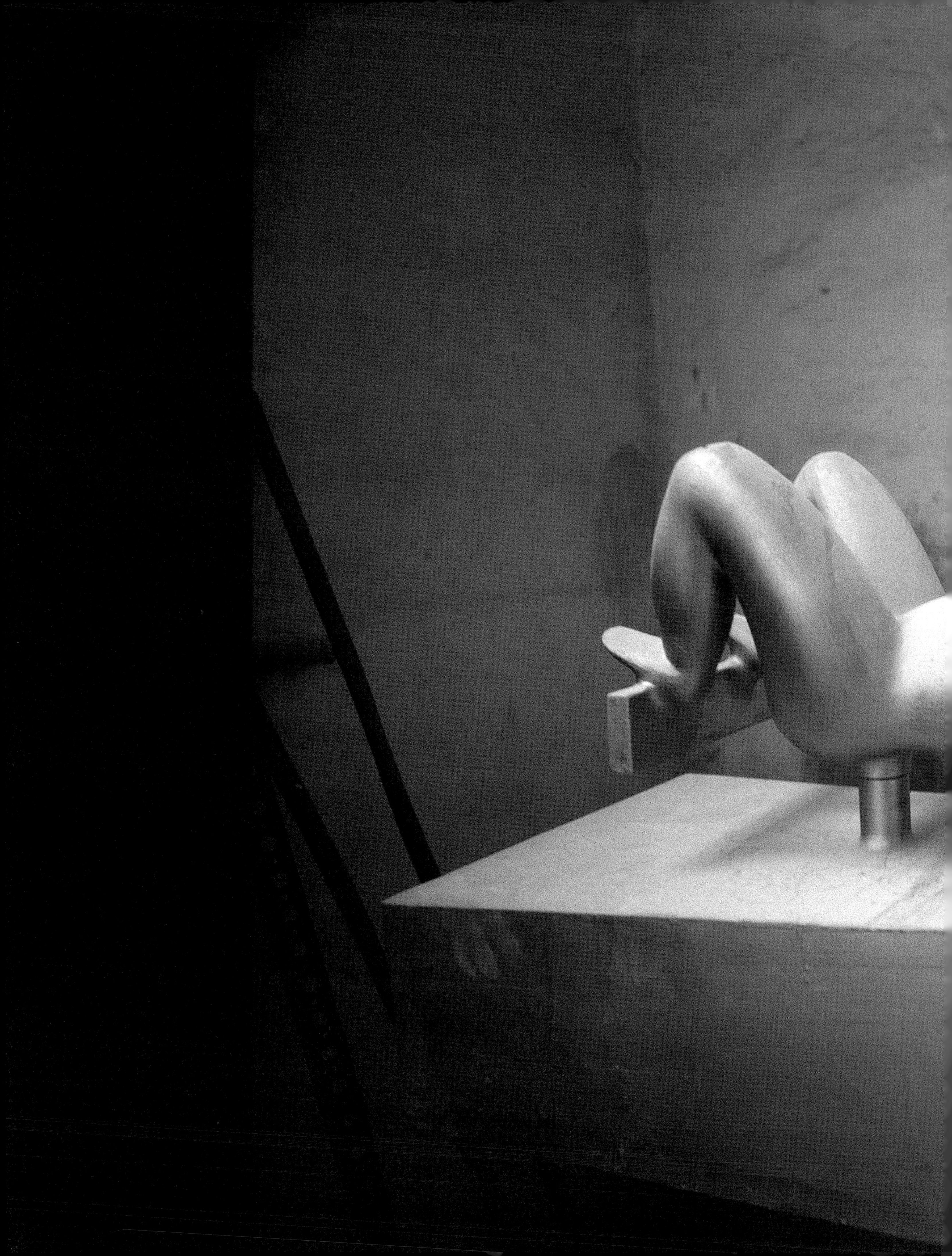

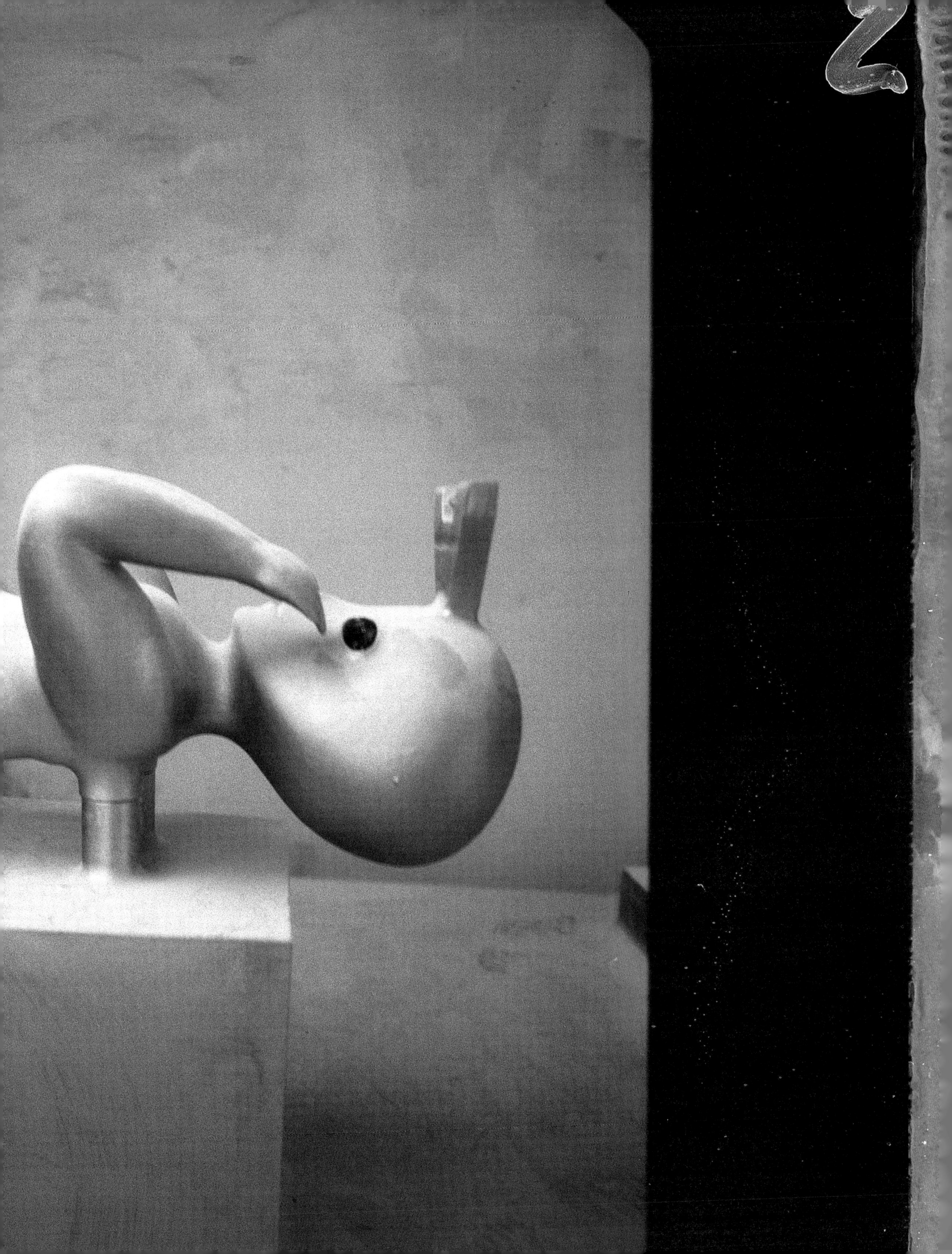

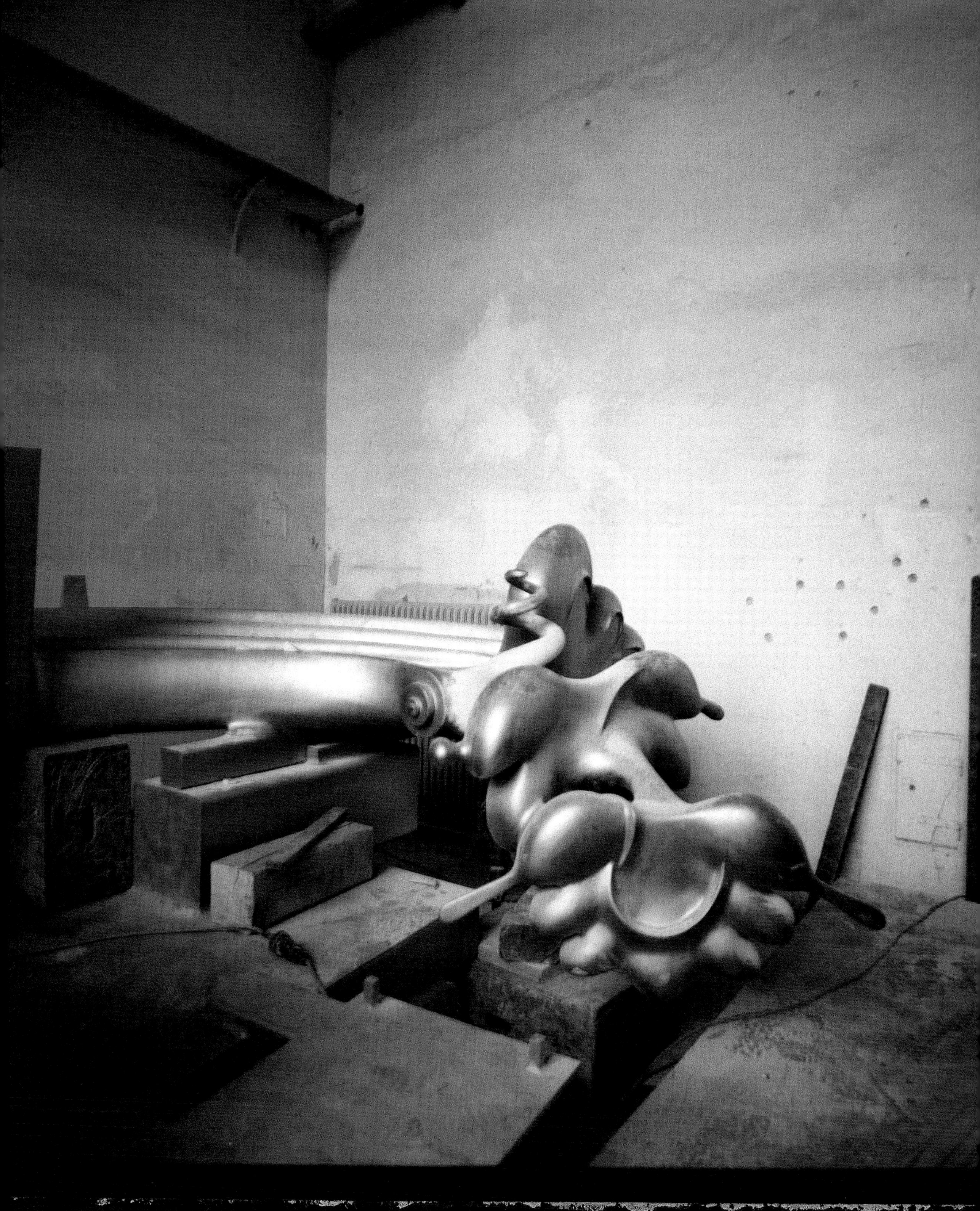

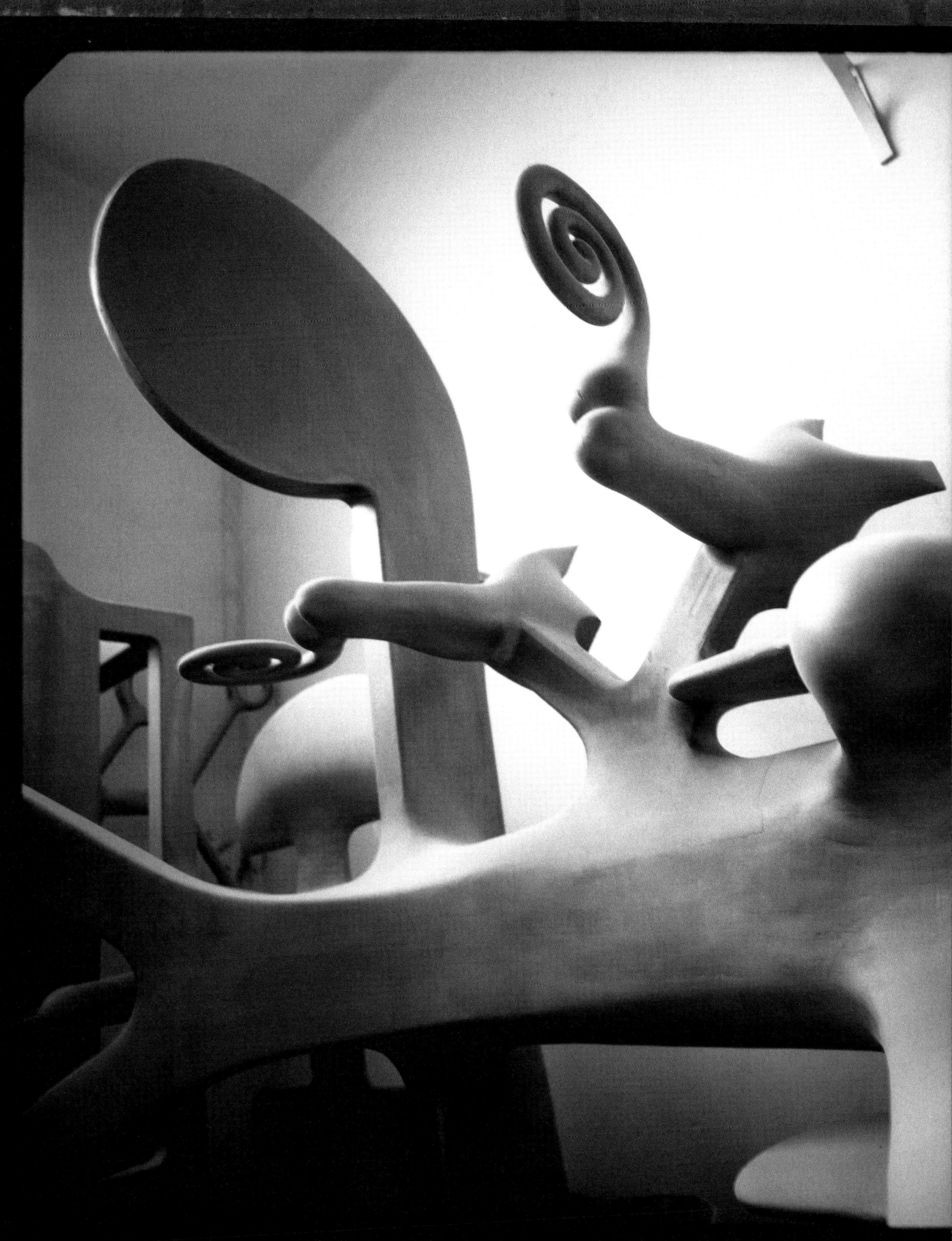

1996 **Jenny Holzer**
New York

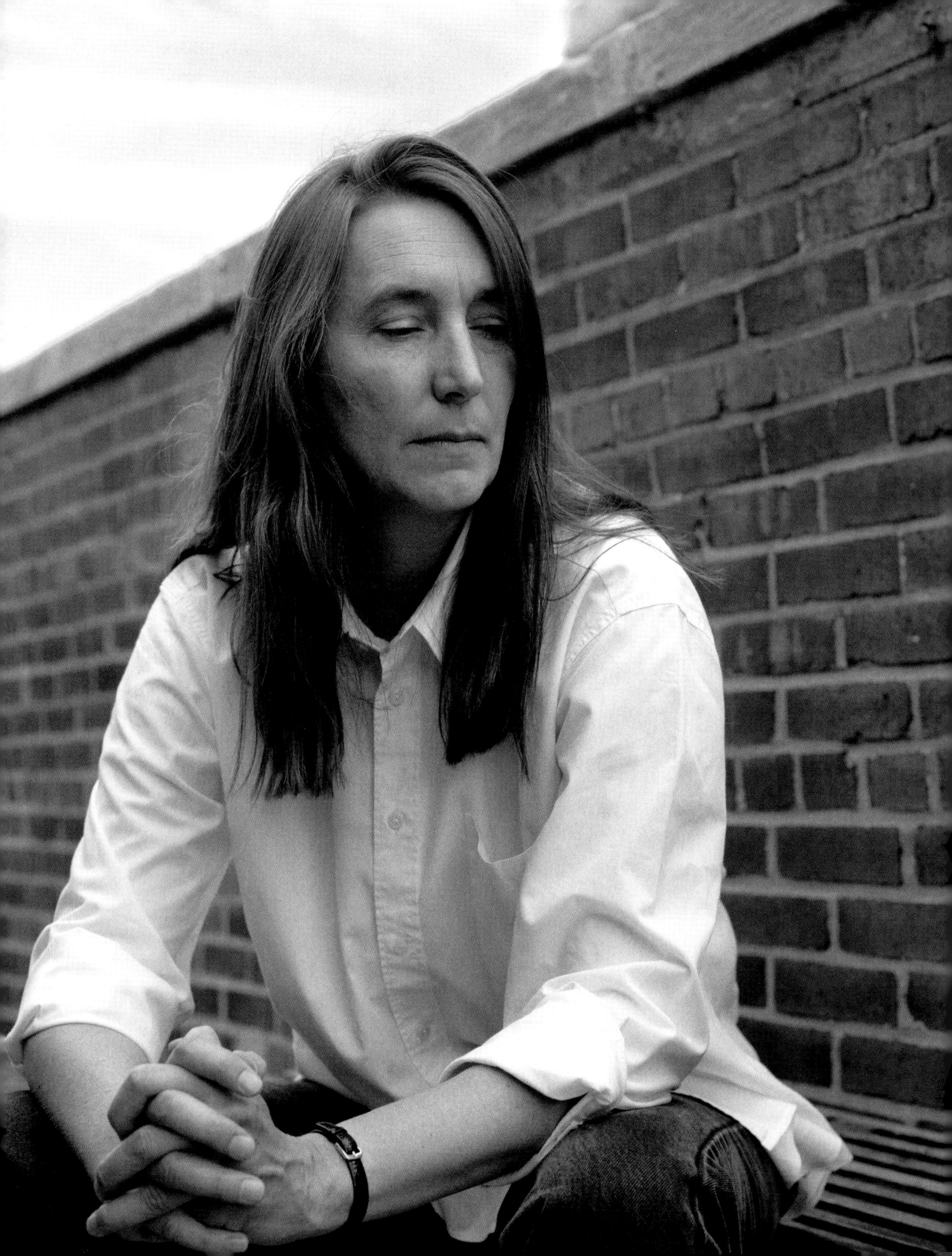

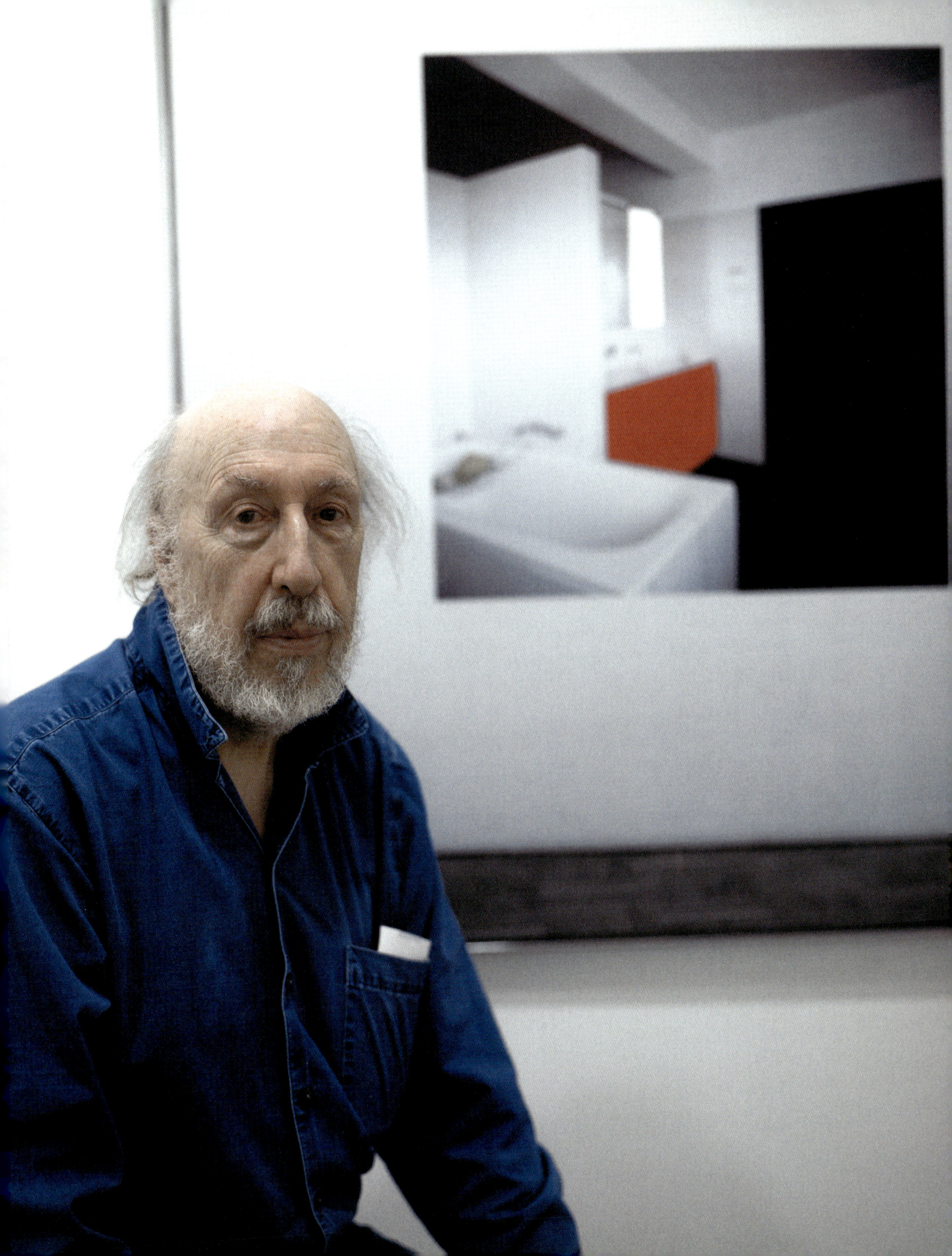

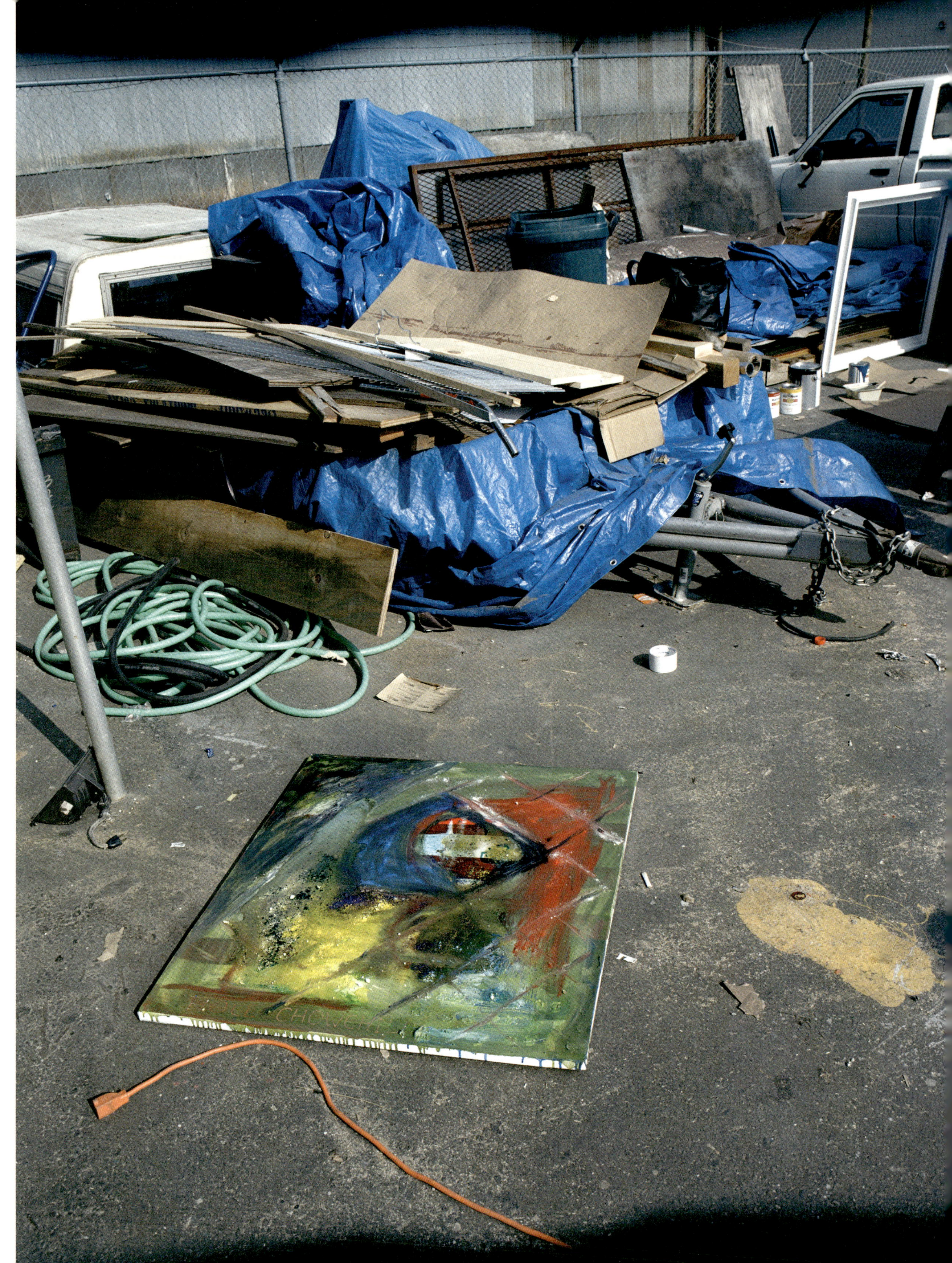

2006 **Jason Rhoades Studio**
Los Angeles

2006 **Jason Rhoades**
Palm Springs

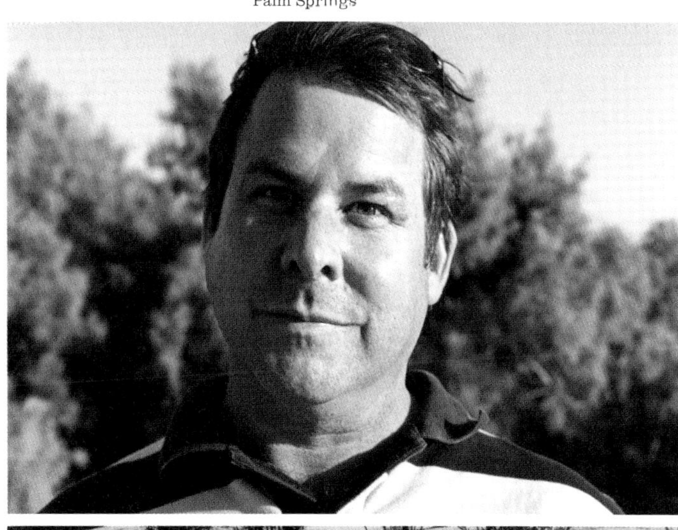

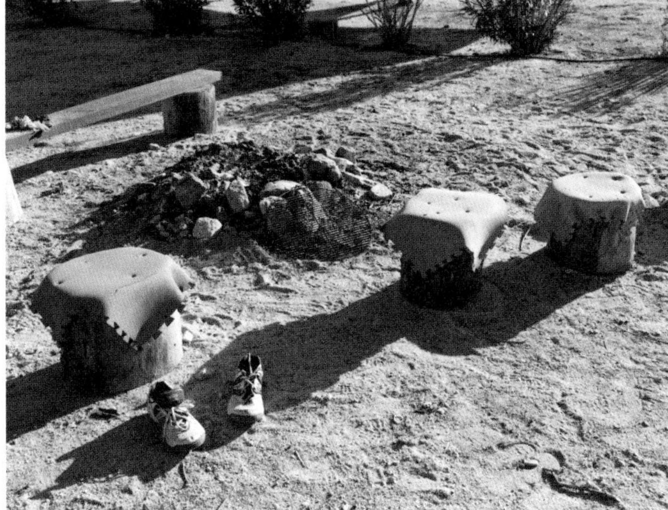

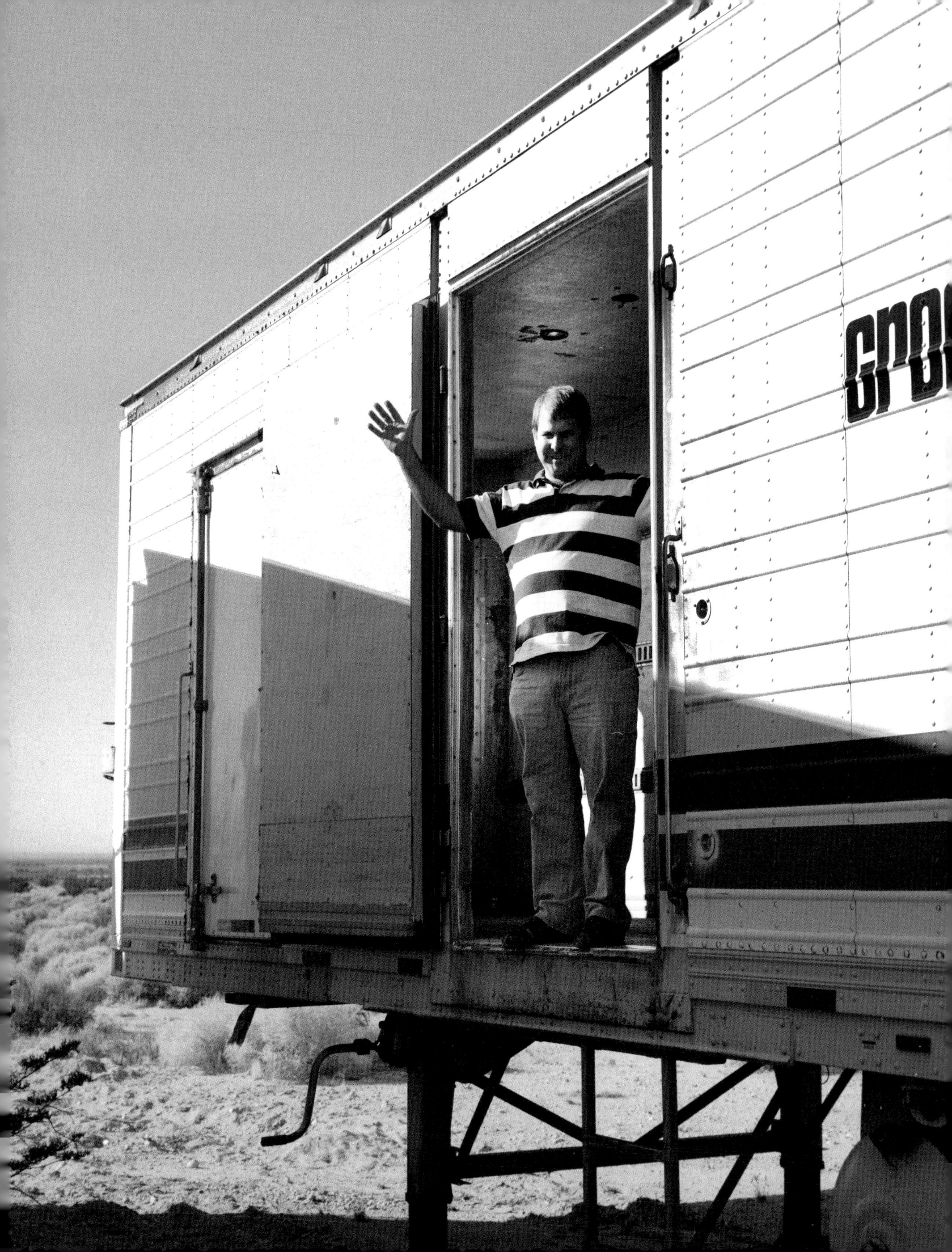

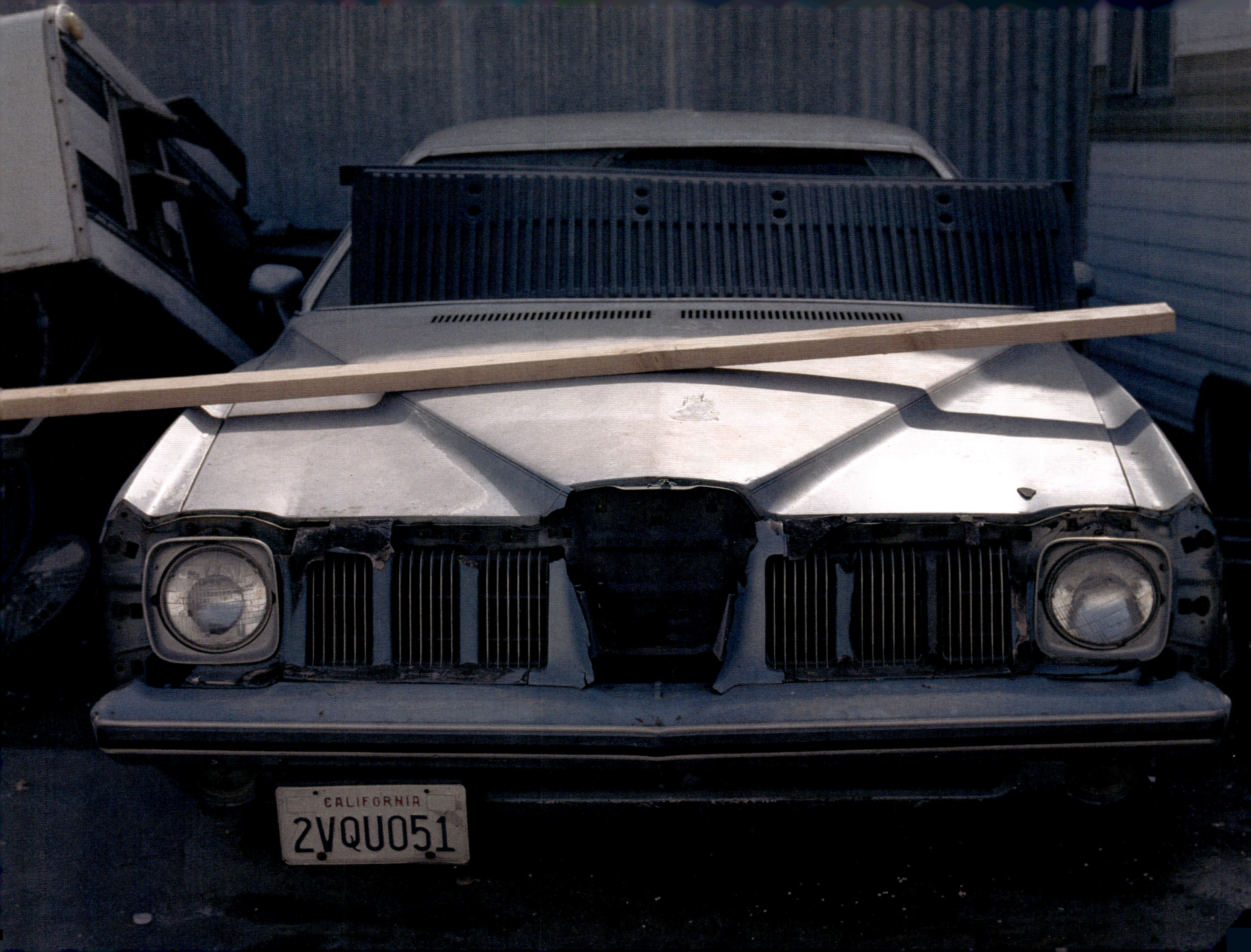
CALIFORNIA
2VQU051

Elfie Semotan

Ausstellungen und Publikationen

Exhibitions and Publications

Ausstellung, Galerie im Taxispalais, Innsbruck – Vitrinen **Einzelausstellung, Semper Depot, Wien** **Buch, „Hair“**	**1976**	Exhibition, Galerie im Taxispalais, Innsbruck – Vitrines Solo Exhibition, Semper Depot, Vienna Book, “Hair”
Einzelausstellung, Café Stein, Wien	**1988**	Solo Exhibition, Café Stein, Vienna
Gruppenausstellung, Nolan/Eckman Gallery, New York **Einzelausstellung, Gabriele Senn Galerie, Wien** **Gruppenausstellung, Schloss Goldegg, Österreich**	**1997**	Group Show, Nolan/Eckman Gallery, New York Solo Exhibition, Gabiele Senn Galerie, Vienna Group Show, Schloss Goldegg, Austria
L'Atelier Soardi, Nizza, zusammen mit Peter Kogler und Manfred Plottegg **Kunsthaus Bregenz, Kooperation mit Peter Kogler. LIFESTYLE**	**1998**	L'Atelier Soardi, Nice, together with Peter Kogler and Manfred Plottegg Kunsthaus Bregenz, cooperation with Peter Kogler. LIFESTYLE
Einzelausstellung, Galerie WestLicht, Wien **Gruppenausstellung, Smithsonian National Portrait Gallery** **Wanderausstellung durch Nordamerika Sammlung Schürmann**	**2001**	Solo Exhibition, Galerie WestLicht, Vienna Group Show, Smithsonian National Portrait Gallery Travelling Exhibition through North America Schürmann Collection
Gruppenausstellung, Österreichisches Kulturinstitut, New York **Gruppenausstellung, Kunsthalle Krems** **Gruppenausstellung, „Libyen“, Kunstraum Karlsplatz, Wien**	**2002**	Group Show, Austrian Cultural Institute, New York Group Show, Kunsthalle Krems Group Show, “Libyen”, Kunstraum Karlsplatz, Vienna
Ausstellung Café Stein-Summerstage, Café Stein, Wien **Gastprofessorin an der Akademie für Angewandte Kunst, Zentrum für Kunst- und Wissenstransfer, in Wien** **„Mimosen, Rosen, Herbstzeitlosen“, Gruppenausstellung, Kunsthalle Krems**	**2003**	Show at Café Stein-Summerstage, Vienna Guest Professor at the Academy for Applied Arts, Department for Art and Knowledge Transfer, Vienna “Mimosen, Rosen, Herbstzeitlosen”, Group Show, Kunsthalle Krems
Buch, „Libyen“, mit Christian Reder **Einzelausstellung, Joanneum, Graz** **„Transcontinental Nomadenoase“, Gruppenausstellung, Art Basel Miami Beach**	**2005**	Book, “Libyen”, with Christian Reder Solo Exhibition, Joanneum, Graz “Transcontinental Nomadenoase”, Group Show, Art Basel Miami Beach
Gruppenausstellung, “Pose & Sculpture”, Casey Kaplan Gallery, New York **„Gleichschwer“, Einzelausstellung, Künstlerhaus Klagenfurt** **Gruppenausstellung Polaroids und Fotografien. „erwischen“, Galerie der Stadt Wels**	**2006**	Group Show, “Pose & Sculpture”, Casey Kaplan Gallery, New York “Gleichschwer”, Solo Exhibition, Künstlerhaus Klagenfurt Group Show Polaroids and Photographs. “erwischen”, Galerie der Stadt Wels
Einzelausstellung, „Grauer Raum“, Kunstraum Innsbruck, Innsbruck **Buch, „Grauer Raum“** **Einzelausstellung, „New York, Wien, Jennersdorf – Die Schöne Jennersdorferin“, Jennersdorf** **Einzelausstellung, „Shower Geschichten“, Momentum Galerie, Wien** **Gruppenausstellung „Schaurausch“, OK-Centrum, Linz in den Schaufenstern und Plätzen der Linzer Innenstadt**	**2007**	Solo Exhibition, “Grauer Raum”, Kunstraum Innsbruck, Innsbruck Book, “Grauer Raum” Solo Exhibition, “New York, Wien, Jennersdorf – Die Schöne Jennersdorferin”, Jennersdorf Solo Exhibition, “Shower Geschichten”, Momentum Galerie, Vienna Group Show “Schaurausch”, OK-Centrum, Linz in shop windows and public spaces in the city of Linz

Ausstellung, „Augen-echo“, Kurt Kocherscheidt, Malerei; Elfie Semotan, Fotografie, Arp Museum, Bahnhof Rolandseck	**2008**	Exhibition, “Augen-echo”, Kurt Kocherscheidt, Paintings; Elfie Semotan, Photography, Arp Museum, Bahnhof Rolandseck
Einzelausstellung, „Male Gestures“, Galerie für Modefotografie, Berlin		Solo Exhibition, “Male Gestures”, Galerie für Modefotografie, Berlin
Gruppenausstellung, Eröffnung der Galerie Capitain und Petzel, Berlin		Group Show, opening show of Galerie Capitain und Petzel, Berlin
Einzelausstellung, Gabriele Senn Galerie, Wien	**2009**	Solo Exhibition, Gabriele Senn Galerie, Vienna
Elfie Semotan & Martin Kippenberger, Galerie Capitain und Petzel, Berlin		Elfie Semotan & Martin Kippenberger, Galerie Capitain und Petzel, Berlin
Einzelausstellung, Galerie Gisela Capitain, Köln	**2010**	Solo Exhibition, Galerie Gisela Capitain, Cologne
Einzelausstellung, Museum der Moderne Rupertinum, Salzburg		Solo Exhibition, Museum der Moderne Rupertinum, Salzburg
Lebt und arbeitet in New York, Wien und Jennersdorf		Lives and works in New York, Vienna and Jennersdorf (Austria)

Special thanks to:
Albert Handler, Sarah Horvath, Ivo Kocherscheidt, Roberto Ohrt und Margit Zuckriegl, ohne deren Einsatz dieses Buch nicht möglich gewesen wäre / without whose efforts this book would not have been possible

Impressum

Dieses Buch erscheint anlässlich der Ausstellung

„Elfie Semotan. Künstlerporträts",
24. Juli – 24. Oktober 2010

This book is published on the occasion of the exhibition

"Elfie Semotan. Portraits of Artists"
24 July – 24 October 2010

Museum der Moderne Salzburg
Rupertinum

Herausgeber / Editor
Museum der Moderne Salzburg
Direktor / Director
Toni Stooss
Autoren / Authors
Roberto Ohrt, Margit Zuckriegl
Übersetzungen / Translations
Deutsch–Englisch / German–English
Jeanne Haunschild
Lektorat / Copy-editing
Sophie Reinhardt
Korrektorat / Proofreading
Brigitte Beier / Stephen Locke
Gestaltung und Satz / Graphic design and typesetting
Albert Handler, moodley brand identity GmbH, Wien
Lithographie / Lithography
Reproline Genceller, München
Papier / Paper
Garda Pat 13 Kiara, 150g/m^3
Druck und Bindung / Printed and bound by
Printer Trento s.r.l, Trento
Printed in Italy

Bibliografische Information der Deutschen Nationalbibliothek

Die Deutsche Nationalbibliothek verzeichnet diese Publikation in der Deutschen Nationalbibliografie; detaillierte bibliografische Daten sind im Internet über http://dnb.d-nb.de abrufbar.

Bibliographic information published by the Deutsche Nationalbibliothek

The Deutsche Nationalbibliothek lists this publication in the Deutsche Nationalbibliografie; detailed bibliographic data are available in the Internet at http://dnb.d-nb.de.

Erschienen bei / **Published by**

Hirmer Verlag München
Nymphenburger Str. 84
80636 München

ISBN 978-3-7774-3291-5 (Softcover)
ISBN 978-3-7774-3331-8 (Hardcover)
ISBN 978-3-7774-3341-7 (Collector's Edition)

www.hirmerverlag.de